'n these uncertain times, now, more than ever, people need
formation, advice and guidance to help them understand what
·y need to do to plan for their retirement. Publications that
ide further insight should be welcomed.'

· **Thoresen, author of the *Thoresen Review of Generic**
*incial Advice***

' *to Beat the Pensions Crisis* should give people more confidence
t what they need to do to plan their retirement finances.'

**Boardman, Visiting Professor at the Pensions Institute, Cass
ıess School**

book is an excellent and much needed practical guide for
· thinking of retirement and planning for it.'

**ı Redman, joint author of *100 Years of the State Pension:
ning from the Past***

le it's great news that we are living longer these days, improved
evity has actually contributed to the pensions crisis. This book
·ibes why in a clear way and, more importantly, explains what
ple can do about it.'

ıul Sweeting, Longevity Strategist, Munich Re

'In the pensions industry we all know about the pensions crisis –
and we are concerned that people haven't understood its full
implications. *How to Beat the Pensions Crisis* does a great job in
explaining what is going on and what people can do about it in a
straightforward and understandable way.'

Ronnie Bowie, President, Faculty of Actuaries

'It's an interesting, easy and important read – I think it's just what
the man in the street needs.'

Joe Chiaro, (ng

D1077223

Beat the
Pensions Crisis

FT Prentice Hall
FINANCIAL TIMES

In an increasingly competitive world, we believe it's
quality of thinking that gives you the edge – an idea that
opens new doors, a technique that solves a problem, or
an insight that simply makes sense of it all. The more
you know, the smarter and faster you can go.

That's why we work with the best minds in business and
finance to bring cutting-edge thinking and best learning
practice to a global market.

Under a range of leading imprints, including *Financial
Times Prentice Hall*, we create world-class print
publications and electronic products bringing our
readers knowledge, skills and understanding, which can
be applied whether studying or at work.

To find out more about Pearson Education publications,
or tell us about the books you'd like to find, you can
visit us at
www.pearsoned.co.uk

Beat the
Pensions Crisis

what you need to do now to improve
your financial future

Brian Wood and Claire Brinn

**Financial Times
Prentice Hall
is an imprint of**

Harlow, England • London • New York • Boston • San Francisco • Toronto • Sydney • Singapore • Hong Kong
Tokyo • Seoul • Taipei • New Delhi • Cape Town • Madrid • Mexico City • Amsterdam • Munich • Paris • Milan

PEARSON EDUCATION LIMITED

Edinburgh Gate
Harlow CM20 2JE
Tel: +44 (0) 1279 623623
Fax: +44 (0) 1279 431059
www.pearsoned.co.uk

First published in Great Britain in 2009
© Pearson Education Limited 2009

The rights of Brian Wood and Claire Brinn to be indentified as authors of this
work have been asserted by them in accordance with the Copyright, Designs
and Patents Act 1988.

ISBN: 978-0-273-72205-2

British Library Cataloguing-in-Publication Data
A catalogue record for this book is available from the British Library

Library of Congress Cataloging-in-Publication Data
A catalog record for this book is available from the Library of Congress

10 9 8 7 6 5 4 3 2 1
13 12 11 10 09

Contents

List of figures

Acknowledgements

Although the pensions crisis is real, it certainly hasn't been created by the pensions industry. One of the pleasures of writing this book has been the positive and helpful reception we have received from people who know about pensions. They are all too aware of the crisis and are concerned that very few members of the public appreciate its impact. Whenever we have asked for help we have received it – and we have asked far too many times to mention everyone. So if you are one of those many people who have assisted us during the writing, please accept our thanks – and also our apologies for not having the space to mention all of your names.

We were not experts on pensions when we started this project, and we could not have completed it without the active contributions of the many people who are. Particular thanks go to Stewart Ritchie, Tom Boardman, Trevor Gosney, Jim Roberts, Ian Costain, Paul Riddell and Andy Dilley. Thanks to Alec Macallan, Sue Brader, Jo Saker and Andrew Saker for their detailed comments on the draft from an employer's perspective. Thanks also to Neil Hobden and Les Sharpe for their help with research.

We are grateful to Robin Prior for coming up with the original concept and for his work in getting the project up and running. Thanks also to Liz Gooster at Pearson Education for spotting the opportunity to create an accessible book on pensions, and to Chris Cudmore and his team for helping us through the writing and editing process.

Last but not least, thanks to our families for putting up with the times that writing the book meant we couldn't be with them fully – and a special mention for Alastair Wood for his assistance with referencing.

Introduction

There is a crisis in pensions today which affects the majority of people in the UK – and this probably includes you.

It's a national crisis that will eventually change the way that our economy, and our whole society, works. You may have heard rumblings in the national press, but would struggle to say what specific impact it will have on your own future.

This book breaks through the complexity surrounding pensions to explain how the crisis affects you, personally, and describes the practical steps that you can take to deal with it.

In this short introductory chapter we start by providing a brief description of the pensions crisis and why it has come about. We set out our objectives for the book, and provide some guidance on how to use it.

Later on we provide a lot more information about the mechanics of the pensions crisis, what impact it has on you, and what actions you can take.

The reality of the pensions crisis

This following example is by no means extreme.

Not so long ago, a male professional in his mid-50s, earning a salary of £60,000, could look forward to retiring on a pension of the equivalent of between £30,000 and £40,000 a year – at age 60 or possibly earlier – having been in final salary schemes for most of his career.

Contrast this with the situation today of a man who is aged 55 and earning £60,000. He has worked all his adult life and paid into money purchase pensions since he was 25, but if he retires at age 60 he would only get the equivalent of about £10,000 a year, an income that would require a radical reduction in his lifestyle. If he decided to retire later at age 65, he might be able to increase his pension to the equivalent of £15,000 a year on the same basis.

What is the pensions crisis? Put simply, the amount of money that we will need in retirement is getting larger, while at the same time the amount of money we are likely to receive is getting smaller – in some cases dramatically so.

There are two fundamental causes: we are living longer after retirement, and investment returns are lower than that in the past. As a result, for most of us a 'pension gap' has opened up – a gap between the amount of pension we would like to receive in retirement, and the amount of pension we will actually get.

At first glance the gap can look large, and it may be tempting to think that the situation is hopeless. A key theme of this book is that we actually have a lot more control than we might have thought. By taking the right actions at the right time, we can do a lot to reduce the size of our pension gap.

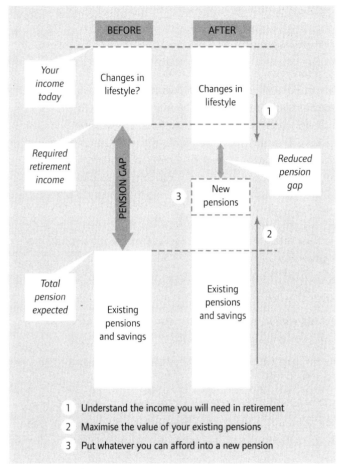

FIGURE 1.1: Reducing your pension gap

When you look at the first column in Figure 1.1 and see the gap, your first reaction might be that your only option for reducing the gap is to try and buy more pensions to fill it. Given that the cost of pensions has increased so much this looks like an incredibly expensive and, for many, impossible proposition.

The gap can be reduced, first, by thinking seriously about what your income needs will really be in retirement – and taking steps to plan for an adjustment if necessary. Although you need to be concerned about increased costs like healthcare, many of your fixed costs like travelling to work, mortgage interest, and pension contributions will cease.

And second, we all have some form of pensions in place already – whether from the state, our current employer, past employers, other pension plans and other assets and savings. By paying attention to the decisions we make around these we can maximise their value and make a significant reduction in our pension gap without having to pay extra. This book covers many such decisions, but the most obvious examples might include:

- using as many available tax reliefs on pensions and savings as possible;
- shopping around for the best pension annuity at retirement rather than accepting the first one you are offered;
- making sure you join a company pension scheme if your employer makes a contribution;
- planning to retire later in exchange for a significant increase in your pensions.

And finally, we need to think about whether we can afford to invest more in pensions. Have they become so expensive that they are not worth investing in? Not at all. Even when interest rates are low, the longer you invest the more your money will grow, so the key point is that you need to start building your pension with a much greater sense of urgency.

The pension gap is real, but by taking the actions described in this book you can gain control and start taking steps to beat the pensions crisis and improve your financial future.

Our objectives

This book has three very specific objectives:

1. to convince you that there are good reasons why you should be worried about your pension;

2. to demonstrate that despite this, all is not lost – you can start to take control of your own future retirement;

3. To provide a practical toolkit for the many things you can do, and decisions you can take, to improve your situation and reduce your pension gap.

Providing for your retirement is simple in concept – money is put away now so it it available to you later when you have given up work. But over time, this simple concept has been surrounded by huge and intimidating complexities.

To achieve our objectives we will need to break through some of the technical mumbo-jumbo that surrounds pensions and explain what is going on in a straightforward way.

We will tell you the basics – what you need to know to take control and start dealing with your own pensions crisis. But we will not attempt to tell you absolutely everything there is to know about pensions.

Rather than clutter the book with all the facts and figures that you might possibly need, we have a companion website – **www.thepensionscrisis.com** – which contains links to a huge variety of online information so that you can rapidly find the latest and most relevant information.

The pensions crisis is a fact of life and it probably affects you. More than anything else, this book is about handing control back to the only person who can really do anything to improve your situation. That's you.

Facts and figures

Too many facts and figures can be confusing, so we have tried to limit ourselves to a small number of examples that reinforce the important points we are making.

*Where there is more information available, we have provided links on our companion website, **www.thepensionscrisis.com**. By using the website, you can also be sure that you are accessing the most up-to-date information.*

The book and the website draw on many sources of information, including government departments and agencies, charities and commercial organisations. We do not have any direct links with any of these bodies, but do appreciate their assistance in making the information available.

How to use this book

Although this book has been arranged in logical sections, you don't need to read them sequentially. Feel free to dive right into the section that is of most interest and jump about to pick up any other information that you need.

There are four main sections:

1 The pensions crisis – explains how the pensions crisis has come about, and explores some of the false beliefs that stop people from taking control of their own future. In doing so, it also outlines the basic mechanics of how pension schemes work.

2 A pensions primer – inside information about pensions that will help you understand the full implications about the choices you have – and make better decisions about them.

3 A practical toolkit – typical issues and options relating to each life stage, together with tips and suggestions about what you can do to start closing your own pension gap. You will want to focus on your present life stage first, but you will also find it illuminating to understand the options available at other stages – particularly if you haven't got there yet.

4 The bottom line – a summary of the key themes for everyone to think about, and some observations about what is likely to happen with the pensions crisis in future.

This book and you

The information in this book was accurate at the time we wrote it and will give you a useful framework for sorting out your own pensions crisis.

However, a book by its very nature cannot provide personalised financial advice. Pensions are a specialist area and can have a huge impact on your life so this is an area where you might well need to consult a professional financial adviser. Chapter 12 gives you some pointers should you decide to do so.

Summary

▌ There is a national crisis in pensions, which probably affects you personally.

▌ The crisis affects you by creating a gap between the pension you would like or expect, and the pension you will actually get.

▌ This book will help you to beat the pensions crisis by showing you what you can do to reduce your pension gap.

part 1

The pensions crisis

In this section we explain how the pensions crisis has come about, and explore some of the false beliefs that stop people from taking control of their own future. In doing so, we also outline the basic mechanics of how pension schemes work.

What pensions crisis?

This chapter outlines the main reasons for the emergence of the pensions crisis, and how most of us are affected.

Pensions cost more than they used to

There are lots of reasons for the emergence of the pensions crisis, but there are two main ones: people are living longer, and investment returns have dropped.

Because of continuing improvements in health we are living much longer than we used to. The positive side is that we can expect to live much longer in retirement. But because we are living longer, our retirement will cost more in total. In financial terms, pensions are therefore much more expensive than they used to be, simply because they will have to pay out for longer than they used to.

Interest rates and investment returns are much lower than they have been for several decades. Pensions plans are essentially a type of saving for the future, and the interest (or investment returns) are added to help buy a larger pension than if the cash were kept under your mattress. Because interest rates are now lower, this effect is reduced and every pound invested in a pension plan will grow less over time and buy a smaller pension.

There are other factors which have made things even worse and we will explore these in a moment. For now, let's just look at these two main causes of the pensions crisis.

Life expectancy

According to official statistics, UK life expectancy has nearly doubled over the past 150 years, increasing by 2 to 2.5 years a decade on average. These improvements have consistently exceeded official projections.

Based on mortality rates in 2004–06, a 65-year-old UK male pensioner is likely to live a further 16.9 years on average, whereas a 65-year-old female pensioner is likely to live 19.7 years.

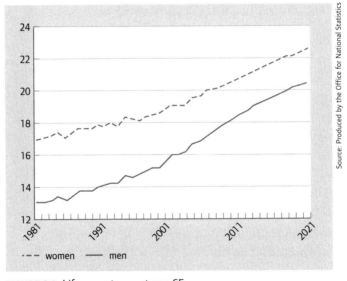

Source: Produced by the Office for National Statistics

FIGURE 2.1: Life expectancy at age 65

Average number of expected years until death at age 65. Based on historical mortality rates from 1981 to 2006 and assumed calendar year mortality rates from the 2006-based principal projections.

> ▌ By July 2008 there were almost 12 million pensioners in the UK – about one-fifth of the population.
>
> ▌ There are 20.5 million people aged over 50 – over one-third of the total UK population.
>
> ▌ The number of people aged 65 or over is expected to rise by over 60% in the next 22 years to almost 15.8 million in 2031.
>
> (Age Concern Report: Older People in the UK – Key Facts & Statistics 2008)

Interest

Interest rates are the 'engine' that drive saving for pensions. We are not going to go into a huge amount of theory but the basic concept, which everyone knows, is that if you invest money you generally expect to get your money back later with interest. But what a lot of people don't fully appreciate is that if you reinvest your money *and the interest you have already received*, the next time around you will get your money back, plus interest, *plus interest on the old interest you have reinvested*. This effect, which is called 'compound interest', looks quite modest in the short term but over a long period it can make a dramatic difference to the amount that is built up (see Figure 10.1 on page 151). Compound interest over a long period is one of the key factors to making pensions affordable, and that's why changes in interest rates are so important in understanding the pensions crisis.

Over the last couple of decades, interest rates in the economy have fallen. In reality there is no single universal interest rate. The one most commonly referred to in the press is the Bank of England's base rate – this is actually a specialist measure of short-term interest rates and can be quite volatile.

There is no universal interest rate for pensions either, but the yield on 20-year government stock is a reasonable indicator when looking at trends. Twenty years is a crude average of the period that people will have to invest for their retirement (from age 45 to 65, say), and also a crude average of the period after retirement (from age 65 to 85, say).

As well as buying government stock, most pensions have also invested in the stock exchange for long-term returns. The FTSE indices are the most commonly used measure of stock exchange performance, but they only measure the price of shares rather than the whole investment return.

Even for stock exchange shares, the yield on government stock is a relevant indicator of broad trends because anyone buying shares will also have an eye on the secure returns from government stock and buy them instead if the returns on shares look too low.

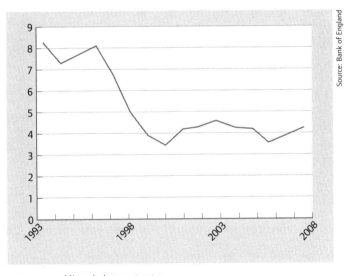

Source: Bank of England

FIGURE 2.2: Historic interest rates
Annual average percentage yield from British Government Securities, 20-year Nominal Implied Forward.

So as we can see, in recent times the general level of interest rates (and, by inference, investment returns) has fallen. If you had invested in 20-year gilts in the early 1990s you would have got a return of about 8% a year. If instead you had invested in the early 2000s, your return would have fallen to roughly 4% a year.

A sum of £10,000 invested in the early 1990s would have received interest of £800 in the first year (and increasing amounts in subsequent years because of the 'compounding' effect – £10,800 rather than £10,000 is invested in the second year, and so on). The sum of £10,000 invested in the early 2000s would have received interest of £400 in the first year, and so on.

These interest rates look quite small, but over time they can make a big difference to the growth of money in a pension. At 8%, an investment would take roughly 9 years to double in value from £10,000 to £20,000. At 4%, it would take roughly 18 years to double in value.

Interest and investments

This issue of interest rates, the stock exchange and different types of investment is a massive subject in itself and well beyond the scope of this book. We have just described the bare minimum to enable you to understand why the pensions crisis has come about.

If you want to know more, there are a number of books which explain investments from the layperson's point of view. We list some of these at our website, www.thepensionscrisis.com.

The combined effect of increased life expectancy and reduced interest rates on pensions can be dramatic – and frightening. Take a simple example (we deliberately haven't allowed for inflation, to keep it simple). If you were a man aged 50 in the 1970s and had £100,000 invested in a pension plan, you might reasonably have expected for this to grow and produce a (level) pension of £50,000 a year when you retired at age 65. Seems like excellent value. Today, to produce a pension of £50,000 a year over the same period, you may need over £300,000 invested – so in this example, the cost of the pension has effectively tripled!

The long-term buying power of pensions is greater today than it used to be, because inflation is lower than it was in the 1970s. Despite this, pensions are still more expensive than they used to be.

Why do I need a pension at all?

Many of us grew up in the years of the Welfare State in the UK. We were led to believe that the Welfare State was capable of providing for all of our health, care and pensions needs. The memory still lingers, even though the State pension has drifted down so much in real value that it can now only be considered as a 'safety net' for those on low incomes.

The boom in generous company pension schemes perpetuated the belief that we would be looked after in retirement. This is simply not the case. If you want a comfortable retirement you will need to look after yourself – whatever your age.

The impact of the crisis on different types of pension

Pensions come from three main sources: the government, companies, and personal pension plans. We will explain the detailed implications of pensions from these sources later on in Chapter 5.

For now, we need to understand that there are two different types of pension: pensions where the amount you get is driven by how much you put in, and pensions where the amount is driven by a set of rules when you retire (irrespective of how much, or little, you have put in).

Source of pension	Pension amount determined by contributions?	Pension amount determined by rules?
State	No	Yes
Company	Yes – 'money purchase' scheme	Yes – 'final salary' scheme
Personal	Yes – always	No

FIGURE 2.3: Types of pension

Pensions where the amount you receive depends on the contributions made (together with investment growth and the cost of buying your pension) are called 'money purchase'. These are the simplest types to understand, because they operate much like a savings account – you put money in, hopefully it grows in value, and then it purchases a pension when you retire. Personal pensions always operate in this way – and some company schemes do. (These are sometimes called 'defined contribution' pensions, but we will use 'money purchase' because we think it is clearer).

The second type are pensions where your entitlement to pension is not finally worked out until you actually retire. For example, although we all make contributions into the state pension scheme, these contributions aren't kept as a separate savings pot in our name. The level of state pension that you actually receive will be determined by the Government when you actually retire.

Company pensions can be of either type. A company pension scheme that is money purchase simply accumulates all the contributions (both yours, and company contributions made on your behalf) into an investment pot that is used to buy your pension when you retire. Alternatively, you may be lucky enough to be in a 'final salary' scheme – where no matter what level of contributions you have made, the scheme will provide a pension equal to a proportion of your salary just before you retire. Sometimes these are called 'defined benefit' schemes to contrast with 'defined contribution' schemes, but we will continue to call them 'final salary' to avoid getting them mixed up.

We will go into a fuller explanation of how these different types of pension work later, in Chapter 5. For now, we will just describe how they have been affected by the pensions crisis. The amount you will get from each and any one of these will probably be less than what you are expecting. Let's look at each in turn to understand why.

Personal pensions

Although the government is keen for us all to put as much as possible into our own pensions, the impact of the pensions crisis on personal pensions has probably caused the greatest damage to individuals (rather than damage to companies). There are two reasons for this.

First, the main feature of a personal pension (which we will describe in more detail later on) is that you, rather than your employer or the government, personally own your pension plan. This has lots of advantages in terms of security and control, but it has one big disadvantage: if a pension gap opens up (and it probably has), it is totally up to you to do something about it. The pensions crisis has done a lot of damage to state pensions and company pensions, but at least there is someone else (either the government or the company) who will be helping to foot the bill. If you have a personal pension, you are on your own.

Second, over time governments have effectively made personal pensions more expensive by gradually diluting the effect of tax relief. The net effect is that every pound going into a personal pension buys less than it used to, tending to increase the pension gap even more for owners of personal pensions.

Company pensions

Most company pension schemes were originally set up as final salary schemes. As we mentioned earlier this meant that, irrespective of changes in investment returns or how long you might live, the pension scheme guaranteed to pay a pension equal to a proportion of your salary just before you retired – hence 'final salary'. The longer you worked in the company, the higher the proportion of final salary. Most final salary pension schemes were set up when there was a legal maximum pension of two-thirds of final salary, and many will still have rules that reflect this limit.

All company pensions suffer from the increased cost of pensions caused by increased life expectancy and lower interest rates in exactly the same way as with personal pensions. The money the company invests towards your pension grows more slowly than it used to and has to stretch over a longer period of time. The big difference is that in a final salary scheme your employer, rather than you, has to foot the bill. That's because the employer has guaranteed to pay a pension based on your final salary, irrespective of how the pension fund performs or how much pensions cost at the time.

The employer's dilemma has been made even worse by the combined impact of higher taxation and tougher regulations, which increase employer costs even further. Even when an employer wants to look after its pensioners, it has become harder and more expensive for them to do so.

So in recent years many employers have restructured their final salary pension schemes to reduce the crippling costs of running them. Unfortunately the main way to reduce the cost of a pension scheme is to reduce the level of pensions promised to scheme members.

Final salary scheme

The way a pension is calculated in a final salary scheme is determined by the 'accrual rate', which is most commonly either '1/80' or '1/60'. For example if you were in a '1/60th' scheme and your salary before retirement was £60,000, you would get a pension equal to £1,000 (i.e. 1/60th of your annual salary) for every year of eligible service with the company. So if you served 20 years with the company, this scheme would guarantee to pay you a pension of £20,000 a year.

There are two main methods that employers have used to cap the spiralling costs of final salary pensions costs: either closing their schemes to new members or by switching to a money purchase pension scheme for new joiners. It is still relatively unusual for companies to change the benefits or contributions for existing members – but this can happen too.

In a company money purchase scheme, all the money contributed to the scheme either by you or your company goes into a pot designated for you – and when you retire the amount of money in the pot is used to buy a pension. At first glance this seems reasonable. But because your pension is no longer directly linked to your final salary, it's more difficult to predict how much you will get. The amount of pension you receive is pretty much a lottery depending on the amount of money put in, investment returns, and the number of years you are expected to live. In these schemes it's more difficult for you to plan your retirement properly, because you will not know how much pension you will receive until you are nearly retired.

In final salary schemes, the company bears all of the risk and the damaging effect this risk might have on their costs. By contrast in money purchase schemes, you bear all of the risk and the damaging impact that this might have on the amount of your pension. Employer contribution levels in a money purchase scheme are almost always set at a lower rate than in final salary schemes (because employers want to reduce costs), so the eventual amount of your pension will be lower. The result is that company pension schemes, which most people think of as generous and safe, now have many of the disadvantages of a personal pension.

And that's if your company still has a pension scheme at all. In the private sector (i.e. non-government), the total number of company pension schemes open to new members has dropped from 62,100 in the year 2000 to 37,400 in the year 2006. Given that most of us are likely to change our jobs at least once in a career and that when we do we become a new member, the likelihood is that most of us will end up either in a money purchase scheme – or in no scheme at all.

The exceptions, of course, are the people who have careers in the public sector – where pensions are still linked to final salary. If they change jobs, as long as they stay in the public sector they can still join a final salary scheme – and often get full credit transferred from their previous scheme through the Public Sector Transfer Club. Through taxation, the rest of the population pay for the final salary pensions of public sector workers no matter what happens to investment returns or how long they live.

So if company pension schemes are generally worse than they used to be, should you bother about joining yours if you have the chance? In most cases the answer is still 'yes'. If your company makes a contribution (and most do), you would effectively be giving money away by not joining. The ins and outs are explained more fully in Chapter 5.

Money purchase scheme

The way a pension is calculated in a money purchase scheme is determined by the amount of pension that the accumulated contributions made on your behalf will buy when you come to retire. So if your employer contributes 6% and you contribute 4%, 10% of your salary is invested in the pension fund each year in your name.

If your final salary is £60,000 and you contributed at this level for 20 years, your pension could easily be well under £10,000 a year. And unlike a final salary scheme, there are no guarantees about how much you would get until you actually retire.

State pensions

Fortunately we all have the state pension to fall back on – or do we? The basic state pension used to be linked to earnings inflation, but the link was switched to price inflation in 1980. The difference between price inflation and earnings inflation in any one year tends to be small, but the 'drip-drip' effect over several years makes a big difference. If the link to earnings had not been broken in 1980, the basic state pension would have been £136.75 a week by 2006. In practice, it was £84.25.

So in terms of our earnings, which is the yardstick we tend to use when we think of pensions, the state pension has fallen in value in real terms by nearly 40%. It was small enough to start with, and it's even smaller now.

The UK only spends about 5% of GDP (Gross Domestic Product) on state pension benefits – which is considerably less than most other European countries. A total of 1.3 million pensioners in the UK have no source of income other than the state pension and benefits.

For most of us, we will have to look elsewhere if we want to preserve some semblance of preferred lifestyle in retirement.

Retirement hasn't got any less expensive

We have already seen one side of the pensions crisis – that the amount of pensions we probably expected to receive has fallen, in some cases quite dramatically, over time. What about the other side – the cost of retirement?

Inflation

Inflation affects you most if you have a money purchase pension (whether through a personal pension or a company money purchase scheme) for two reasons. First, the value of your contributions, while increasing with interest, is also eroded by inflation each year. (Over long periods interest rates tend to outstrip inflation rates, so on balance you should still expect to get a net positive return.) And second, because you will eventually have to buy your pension at retirement, the cost of 'inflation-proofing' your pension depends on the prospects for future inflation (see Chapter 6 for an example of this).

The impact of inflation is less (for you) on your state pension and if you have a final salary pension. State pensions already have some inflation-proofing – they are linked to the retail price index (which rises slower than earnings inflation). Because final salary schemes relate your pension to your final employed salary, they are effectively inflation-proofed before retirement. And once you retire, some final salary schemes have automatic inflation-proofing – and many others have been in the habit of voluntarily increasing pensions to match inflation.

So the fact that inflation is lower today than historically is a small amount of good news, particularly if you have a money purchase pension. Unfortunately money purchase pensions are precisely the pensions that have been hardest hit by the pensions crisis, so the benefits of lower inflation only makes a modest dent in the scale of the problem.

Lifestyle expectations

Now let's get back to the bad news. Most of us were brought up with the concept that retirement was a time for relative inactivity. We would sit in an armchair by the fire and go for occasional walks, and our financial needs would be modest.

To a certain extent our financial needs will be lower because the shift from working to retirement does have scope for cost reductions – the most obvious one being the cost of travelling to work. But our lifestyle expectations are dramatically different today. We expect to have an active retirement – travelling the world, engaging with our communities and families, while still providing support to our children and grandchildren.

All of this costs money. In financial terms, the effect is that when we move into retirement we don't expect such a sudden step-down in the costs of our lifestyle that were built into assumptions around pensions in the past. The actual impact on you will depend on your personal attitude to retirement, but the overall effect is real.

Cost of healthcare

Even though we probably see the early part of our retirement as active, later on we cannot avoid the fact that we are highly likely to need healthcare. And the older we get, the more likely we are to need it.

The costs of comprehensive healthcare have been going through the roof, partly because more things are treatable (and we increasingly expect them to be treated) and partly because the cost of each treatment gets more and more expensive. The effect is easiest to track when looking at premium rates for private health insurance, but exactly the same pressures continue to increase the total cost of running the National Health Service.

For example, if you were paying £50 a month for health insurance at age 40 this would roughly double to £100 by age 60, triple to £150 by age 70 and quadruple to £200 by age 80!

The NHS also has to cope with paying for more expensive care for relatively more and more people. Today, every 1,000 workers (who are the ones who generate wealth and pay taxes) support about 1,100 non-workers (mainly children and retired people). The number of non-workers is predicted to rise to 1,350 over the next few decades, mainly because of growth in the retired population – this strikes at the heart of how the NHS is funded.

Many of us will have no option but to rely on the NHS as the sole source of our healthcare during our retirement, but this no longer looks like a straightforward option. Buying some form of health insurance looks desirable, but it will be expensive.

Long-term care

The NHS 'fallback' option isn't the full safety net you thought it was either. If you ultimately need to receive long-term care in retirement, the government will only fund the cost of medical provision (unless you are fortunate enough to be living in Scotland – see Chapter 6, page 76) – not the full cost of residential care. You will not have a choice – the local authority is entitled to seize your assets to cover the cost of residential care so only people close to the poverty line will get free care.

About 30% of the current population over age 65 have at least one disability, and 4% reside in either a residential home or nursing home. A recent study by SAGA indicates that residential care can easily cost between £25,000 and £30,000 a year, while 47% of people underestimate this bill by as much as £20,000 a year. Even with that level of error,

57% think it is likely that any potential inheritance will be eaten up funding long-term care. Private nursing care is more expensive, currently averaging £35,000 a year.

Women and the pensions crisis

The pensions crisis is bad enough for men, but it is even worse for women. Despite the fact that women live longer than men by an average of five years, they are far less likely to make adequate provision for their own retirement.

Women and pensions

Only 30% of women currently retired have a full basic state pension.

Only 33% of women reaching retirement age in 2005 qualified for a full pension compared to 85% of men.

Over 60% of pensioners living in poverty are women.

Only 38% of working-age women (47% of men) are contributing to a private pension and they make much lower provision (average £89 per month for women vs £156 per month for men)

Source: Scottish Widows Women and Pensions Report 2008

There are lots of reasons, mostly historic and cultural, why the pension gap is likely to be worse for women:

▌ Women are more likely than men to be in low-paid and part-time work: 40% of women in work are part-timers compared to 11% of men; 29% of women are in low-paid work compared to 16% of men.

▌ Women tend to take more time out of the workforce to have a family. They are twice as likely as men to reduce pension contributions when they start a family.

▌ Women are more likely to take on caring responsibilities, e.g. for elderly parents or in-laws, rather than work.

▌ The state pension system traditionally worked on the assumption that women would be looked after by their husbands in retirement and they were able to contribute a lower rate of NI (married women's rate) to reflect the fact that they would not need to build up their own entitlement.

▌ However, single parents, 90% of whom are women, now make up a quarter of all families.

▌ Women have not been fully aware of the value of pensions as an asset in a divorce. (This is now changing where lawyers are involved, but is still a risk if they are not.)

The cost of your pension

Taking all this into account, roughly how much do you think you might need to live on in retirement? Once you have a figure in mind, have a look at the next table that shows the scale of the total pension pot that you might need to accumulate to afford that amount of pension.

Pension required	£20,000	£40,000	£60,000
Pension fund needed for man aged 65	**£450,000**	**£900,000**	**£1,350,000**
Pension fund needed for woman aged 60	**£600,000**	**£1,200,000**	**£1,800,000**

Source: FSA 'Moneymadeclear' website

FIGURE 2.4: How much pensions really cost
Single life, escalating at RPI, 5-year guaranteed.

This probably looks like a scary amount of money, probably much more than you ever had in mind. That's right at the heart of the problem with pensions today – they are far more expensive than they used to be, and there is no reason to believe that they will start getting cheaper anytime soon.

Your immediate reaction might be that the situation is so bad that you might as well give up. But for a fairly small effort in terms of understanding the pensions crisis you can start to chip away at the problem, often at no cost at all, by making decisions and taking action that move you in the right direction.

The pensions crisis is real

Back in history, when the concept of pensions was first established, the standard retirement age for men was set at 65 (and later, 60 for women) precisely because very few people were expected to live to that age. If you did manage it, you expected to live a modest life – and a short one. In these circumstances a modest amount of pensions provision went a long way.

That's clearly not the case today.

We all now expect to reach retirement age, we expect to lead fulfilling lives in retirement, and we expect to receive whatever healthcare we need. How ironic that just at this positive moment in history when most of us are looking forward to an enjoyable and happy retirement, the pensions that we all took for granted are crumbling away under our feet.

The very fact that we are living longer makes pensions more expensive. Lower interest rates, while positive for the economy, also make pensions more expensive. Successive governments have gnawed away at the state pension and treated company and personal pensions as a soft target to raise taxes. Company pension schemes have been forced to become less generous, particularly for those who choose to change jobs.

All this has happened at a time when our financial needs and wants in retirement are greater than ever before.

This is the pensions crisis. Unless you have been incredibly lucky it affects you, and you need to do something about it. No one else will do it for you.

The positive news is that you have many more choices than you probably thought you did. The obvious one is to invest as much as you can as soon as you can in a pension. But as we will see later, there are a host of other options that can improve the amount of pension you will get when you retire.

Summary

▌ The pensions crisis has emerged over the last few years because:

 – we are all living longer in retirement, so the cost of providing a pension has increased;

 – investing for the future has become more expensive as interest rates and investment returns have dropped.

▌ The most visible effects of the pensions crisis are a sharp increase in the cost of pensions and a decline in the benefits available in company pension schemes.

▌ The only people not affected by the pensions crisis (so far) are people who have had long periods of continuous service in either a generous final salary company pension scheme or who have a public sector pension.

Myths and delusions about pensions

3

This chapter explores some of the myths that have evolved around pensions. We don't think about pensions every day, and for most of us the subject is so big, complex and daunting that it is much easier to live with these myths – even when, deep down in our hearts, we know they are not true. It's a natural way of 'coping' with a difficult subject.

The risk is these myths stop us coming to terms with the reality of what is happening – and what we can do about it.

The major myth: I will probably be OK

The number one myth about pensions, the delusion that we are too frightened to challenge, is that our finances in retirement will probably be fine. But sadly, for most of us, they probably won't.

The reality

'Nearly half of those who could and should be making financial provision for their retirement are not doing enough, and it appears that many are drawing on non-pension savings that may previously have been earmarked for retirement to help tide them through hard times.

> *There remain substantial variations between different groups. Women still lag significantly behind men, although the gap has narrowed. Younger people, despite good intentions, are saving less than those closer to retirement. And defined-benefit (final salary) schemes, which remain the most secure way to build up an adequate pension, are heavily concentrated in the public sector.'*
>
> The Scottish Widows UK Pensions Report 2008

Many of us lived through the post-war world of the 1950s, 1960s and 1970s: a new era of social welfare when the state was expected to provide for our needs when we could no longer do so ourselves. Even people too young to remember these times have grown up in a culture where their parents had faith in the state system and passed this faith on to the family.

This sense of comfort was reinforced by the growth of company pension schemes, which grew from 3.1 million members in 1953 to a peak of 8.1 million in 1967. These schemes were intended to reward employee loyalty during an era where staying with the same company for a long time, possibly for life, was not considered unusual. By 1979, 92% of company schemes were of the most generous 'final salary' type.

Many of the beliefs about social welfare and pensions have persisted even when they are no longer valid. Their existence acts as a barrier to new and more useful beliefs about our society today and how we need to operate within it.

Private pension paupers

'Fidelity International warns of "private pension paupers" as final salary schemes give way to money purchase.

The typical UK worker is on course to retire on just £215 per week, less than half of national average earnings and below the current

▶

> *minimum wage, according to the third annual Fidelity Retirement Index. The index, built on complex financial modelling and a survey of more than 1,000 people, indicates that people are set to see their income drop by 53% on reaching retirement. This figure covers all sources of income, including State pension benefits and private pensions.'*
>
> Fidelity International, May 2008

Myth 2: I can live on the basic state pension

We all know that we are entitled to the state pension and probably comfort ourselves that if all else fails we can live on it. But much of this comfort is misplaced because we don't actually realise just how modest the state pension is compared to our current income.

The insurance company AXA conducted research with volunteers to see how well they would cope when retired if forced to live on just a state pension. They were asked to budget and live on the pension for a week. Although they only researched with twenty-six couples, their findings are likely to be fairly representative. Despite their planning and the fact that it was a one-off exercise, almost everyone found it to be impossible.

> Some of the findings of the research are as follows:
>
> ▍ Single women had overspent their budget by 200%.
> ▍ Couples taking part overspent by 168%.
> ▍ On average, the weekly pension lasted for about three days.
>
> A link to the full report is available on **www.thepensionscrisis.com**.

The report concludes:

'What is quite clear is that the state pension will not suffice for many people. Those wanting any quality of life in retirement must:

▌ make greater provision for themselves;

▌ plan their retirement as early as they can;

▌ understand the limitations of the lifestyle they will be able to afford, and be certain to live within those limitations.'

> The resident independent financial adviser commented on the findings:
>
> 'For those that took part, this experiment has been a real call to action. Many of them had visions of retiring at 55, even though they had no clear idea of how much money they were set to have as a pension. The pensions industry and the government needs to get the message across that it is easier to make some small changes now to set aside long-term savings for retirement than having to make major and uncomfortable changes later on. I feel that our "have it all now" culture means that people are not willing to budget to set aside long term savings. This is likely to lead to a harsh retirement for many people.'

Myth 3: Pensions are too complicated

It's true that there is a lot of complexity surrounding pensions. This complexity starts with the multiple layers of regulation around the tax advantages of pensions, which are then reflected in the bewildering array of pension products and options available. So you have every right to be confused at times.

But the underlying premise is not complicated at all: the more that is saved on your behalf, the greater your income will be in retirement. You can improve the situation by saving more personally, and by taking steps to ensure that your existing pension arrangements and entitlements aren't allowed to leak away. Once you decide to take control in this way, you are a long way towards getting on top of your pensions planning.

Myth 4: You can't trust pensions

Far from it: despite any negative publicity you may hear, a pension is probably the most rock-solid financial investment that is available to you.

The state pension and government pension schemes are backed by taxpayers and the force of law. These pensions will always get paid (although the Government can change the amount that gets paid).

Company pension schemes are protected by their own legislation, and companies have to set up a pension fund that is completely separate from the rest of their assets. Pension funds have got a bad press recently because of the negative impact of the pensions crisis, but there are huge protections in place to make sure that once a pension promise is made by a company pension scheme, it is delivered. The Government has operated the Financial Assistance Scheme since 1997 for people in pension funds that failed to meet their liabilities, and this was superseded in 2005 by the establishment of the Pension Protection Fund – which effectively helps to bail out any schemes that get into serious trouble (but doesn't cover 100% of benefits).

Most personal pension policies are issued by insurance companies. Despite all the changes in the financial services industry in the past 50 years, no pension policy has failed to pay out, because of the highly disciplined and regulated management of life assurance companies. The people who have policies with the troubled Equitable Life will all receive a payout, even if the amount is less than they had been expecting.

No form of investment is ever risk-free, but we don't know of any form of financial investment that is more regulated, or more secure, than a pension.

Myth 5: My house is my pension

Most people see their house as their biggest asset. It is very tangible, and in recent decades property values have risen so rapidly that it looks like a huge store of value. There are major problems with this thinking.

▌ As we will see later, the price of a pension is high – much higher than you probably expect. So, for example, £100,000 of equity in a house might only buy a pension of about £4,000 a year. Looking at this in another way your existing pension arrangements, although they are far less visible, could actually be much more valuable than your house – which is why it is so important to pay attention to them.

▌ Releasing the equity value of the house can be cumbersome and expensive. The simplest method is to sell, but you still have to live somewhere.

▌ We think of the value of a house in terms of the cash equivalent. But when property markets fall, as they have done in 2008 and 2009, it may be extremely difficult to convert a house into cash at all, let alone obtain the value you might have been expecting.

▌ It is likely that you also think of your house as the source of an inheritance for your children. But anything you do to raise cash on the back of your property will also reduce the value of your estate – and possibly even wipe it out.

If you have a house with a high realisable value, you could certainly try and tap into that value to help close your pension gap. But it is unlikely to solve the problem totally.

Myth 6: I'm OK because I am already investing in a pension

You may believe that, because you are currently in a pension scheme or own a personal pension policy, you don't have a problem. But it's quite likely that you do – and the fact that you have made some pension provision may even have made things worse because it lulled you into a false sense of security and prevented you from taking any further action.

Unless you have been in either government or company final salary pension schemes for the bulk of your career, you almost certainly have a pension gap. Later on, we will explain in more detail about how you can work out the size of your pension gap.

A 2008 survey by Prudential showed that voluntary contributions to private and company pension schemes have plummeted by 53% in the previous 18 months as the economic downturn reduced monthly pension savings from an average of £279.38 a month to £129.35 a month – with women saving even less at £74.95 a month. To put this into terms of pensions being bought, in 2007 a premium of £200 per month generated an average fund value of £56,518 in a with-profits pension policy that had been running for 15 years. This would have purchased a pension of £3,840 a year.

Myth 7: My other assets will be enough

The purpose of pensions is to help you provide for a comfortable retirement. All governments, past, present and future, are positive about pensions and wish to promote them. Whatever type of pension you consider, it has three core attributes that all governments have always agreed upon:

1 you have to put money away for the future – and you can't spend that money today;

2 there is a high degree of regulation of your pension to make sure that it actually pays out;

3 your pension money attracts tax relief.

So pension plans have been specially constructed and incentivised to enable you to build an income for your future retirement.

Despite this, you don't *have* to use a pension plan. By keeping money in cash and other assets (other than your pension) you definitely have more flexibility in terms of how you can use and invest your money in the short term. But you do need to be aware of the large difference that tax relief can make. If you plan carefully, you could use individual savings accounts (ISAs) to build up a savings portfolio that eventually attracts tax relief (see page 146 for more information).

The main thing is that although you are free to use non-pension assets to fund your retirement, it is dangerous to assume that they will automatically be enough. You can build up non-pension assets to complement your pension, but would need to exercise care and skill to be able to do without a pension at all.

The power of pensions tax relief

John is a 35-year-old basic-rate taxpayer with £10,000 available to invest. He could save either through a pension or a normal investment bond. If he invests in a pension, he can use his £10,000 to buy a pension plan worth £12,500 because he receives tax relief on his contribution.

▶

> *At age 55 his investment bond would have grown to £21,911 while his pension fund has actually grown to £33,166 (using comparable assumptions on investment returns, but allowing for lower tax on pensions). He takes 25% of his pension fund as tax-free cash (£8,291.50) and uses the remainder to provide a net income of £1,000 a year (a gross drawdown income of £1,250 on which he pays tax). At age 74 his pension fund is still worth £22,940 and he could purchase an annuity to provide a pension for the rest of his life.*
>
> *The investment bond, on the other hand, could have paid out exactly the same net cash amounts (£8,291.50 plus £1,000 net a year) – but would have completely run out at age 74.*
>
> *The accumulated difference of £22,940 at age 74 between the pension and the investment bond has been created purely by the tax relief available on the pension. If John were a higher-rate taxpayer, the difference would be greater.*

Myth 8: It's too late – there is no point

It's true that the earlier you start saving, the greater the impact of growth in your savings on the pension you will receive. But it's never too late.

For every £1 you put into a pension plan now, however close you are to retirement, you are likely to generate more than £1 in spendable cash in your retirement because of the combined impact of investment growth and tax relief. (The one exception to this is if your expected pension is so low that you are likely to be eligible for pension credit – see Chapter 5).

And you can go further than this without spending money by optimising many of the other decisions you make that will affect your pension and income needs. The key is to realise that a laissez-faire approach doesn't work for pensions – if you avoid thinking about your pension you could lose a lot of money unnecessarily. You need to decide to take control now, rather than leaving things to fate.

Summary

▌ There are a number of myths that prevent us from taking control of our pension.

▌ The most damaging myth about pensions is that, somehow, someone else will be taking care of our financial needs in retirement.

▌ In reality, the pensions crisis has created a significant pension gap for most of us.

▌ Practical studies have shown that for most people, living on the state pension is almost impossible.

▌ You can build up tax efficient non-pension assets but you are unlikely to be able to avoid the use of a pension vehicle entirely. It is the most tax efficient route for your pension savings.

part

2

A pensions primer

In this section we provide some inside information about pensions that will help you understand the full implications about the choices you have - and make better decisions about them.

Inside information

We have already said that the huge amount of information available on pensions makes them difficult to understand. In this chapter we pick out just a few key concepts that will enable you to get under the skin of how pensions work, and take control over some of your key decisions. Taking time to get to grips with these represents a fairly small effort for a big potential pay-off.

There are four key concepts that will give you the inside track. They are:

1 Your pension pot – the total amount of money, from whatever source, that you could use to buy a pension.

2 The price of your pension – how much you would need to pay for every £1 of pension income.

3 Your pension gap – the difference between the amount of pension you would like, and the actual amount that you are likely to get.

4 The pension turbocharger – the combination of different effects that could either boost your pension, or decimate it if you make the wrong decisions.

Your pension pot

Your pension pot is the total amount of money from all sources, held in various different places, which will one day be used to provide your income in retirement. Most of this is actually locked away in various pension plans or schemes until you retire – so you can't physically get your hands on your pension pot. It's just a convenient shorthand that will make a lot of our explanations much easier to follow.

We have already described the major ways you are likely to receive a pension, and the individual pots in each of these make up your total pension pot:

- from the state;
- from company pension schemes;
- from personal pension policies;
- from your other assets.

In most cases these individual pots are real cash and investments which are being held so that a pension can be bought for you some day. (The main exception is the state pension, which is backed by a government promise rather than real cash.)

Although it is sometimes useful to know the amount of cash in a single pot, we never really need to calculate the precise amount of your total pension pot. All you need is a rough approximation so you can understand your likely financial situation in retirement. What we are ultimately interested in, after all, is the amount of pension you will get.

So when we use a phrase like the size of your pension pot or refer to changes in your pension pot, this is just a shorthand for totting up the effect across all the individual pots. It is a useful tool for understanding how your choices might affect what really matters: the amount of your pension.

The price of your pension

How do you get from your pension pot to the amount of your pension? When you retire, your pension pot is used to purchase a pension that will be payable to you for the rest of your life. The price of your pension depends on a host of factors which will be discussed in greater detail in Chapter 7. But the main ones are:

- your gender;
- your age at retirement;
- your health;
- the rate at which your pension increases each year (the escalation rate);
- whether your pension is just for you, or needs to last for the lifetime of your spouse too.

For now, the important thing to appreciate is that there is a price for your pension – and it is probably higher than you suspected. As we explained earlier, the main reasons are that people are living much longer than they used to (so the pension pot has to be spread over more expected pension payments) and investment returns are lower than they used to be.

Using your pension price in reverse

Suppose that you have looked at all the options for pensions outlined in Chapter 2, and worked out that you have to pay £25 for every £1 of pension. So a pension pot of £250,000 will buy a pension that starts at £10,000 a year. This was a credible number at the time of writing, but may not be valid today.

In principle, the price of your pension should also work in reverse. In other words, if you're entitled to a pension of £10,000 a year and are being offered cash in exchange for this you should expect to receive about £250,000. The price for going from pension pot to pension amount will never exactly equal the price for the reverse transaction – that is a feature of all markets – but it shouldn't be a million miles away.

Becoming familiar with a rough but fair price for your pension is immensely valuable in understanding some of the choices that will be outlined later on. You can do this by checking the links on our website.

Your pension gap

Because of all the complexities in pensions the precise amount of your pension gap is difficult to calculate accurately, but that doesn't really matter because all you need to make the right decision is a rough indication. It is a crucial concept to understand if you want to have a happy retirement that is not plagued by financial worries.

Put simply, the pension gap is the difference between the pension that you want and the pension that you will actually get, so it is the difference between two numbers.

1. The pension you will need in order to have a comfortable retirement: by definition, this can never be a precise 'calculation', it's more of a rough estimate that you need in order to plan for your retirement properly.

2. The total pension you will be receiving from a variety of different sources: some of these pensions will start at different times and will be paid in different ways, so once again the best you can probably achieve is a rough estimate.

The central theme of this book is that many people currently have a significant pension gap, but just don't realise it – in short, that's what the pensions crisis has caused. The first thing to do to deal with it is work out roughly how big it is (we will show you how to do this in Chapter 6) and then focus on the steps you can take to reduce its size.

The pension turbocharger

One of the most powerful insights into how pensions work is something we will call the 'pension turbocharger'. As you will see, it's called the turbocharger because it can have a major positive (or negative!) impact on the amount of pension that you might receive.

This is how it works. If you have the choice of when to retire and choose to retire later rather than sooner, the amount of pension that you receive could be boosted significantly in a number of different ways. All these factors pull things in the same direction, so when they are combined it's like a turbo boost that magnifies the changes in your pension. Here are these factors:

▌ If you are in a company pension scheme, you continue to increase the size of your pension pot, if your own contributions or company contributions (or both) continue to be made into the scheme.

▌ The amount of money inside your pension pot has the opportunity to grow and attract investment returns for more time before it has to be cashed in to buy a pension.

▌ Since you are retiring later than originally planned, you will receive a smaller number of pension payments over the remainder of your life than you would have done. So every £1 inside your pension pot can buy a higher amount of pension that you will receive each year.

▌ If you are still employed you will be receiving an income which is probably higher than the amount of pension you would have received in retirement. You have the opportunity to reinvest some of the difference to add to your pension pot. This extra amount in your pension pot will buy an extra pension when you do actually retire.

As we will see later in the book, some or all of these conditions may be present depending on the precise situation you are in. Each one of them may look a bit dry and technical, but when they are combined you can get the 'turbo' effect and this can make a huge impact on the pension that you receive. Here is an example.

EXAMPLE

A male aged 60 who has been making pension contributions starting at £1,000 a month for 15 years might retire on a starting pension of £9,200 a year. By waiting to retire at age 65 instead (and continuing to make contributions at a similar level), the starting pension would rise to £16,200 a year. The pension turbocharger increases the pension by 76% over 5 years, or roughly 12% increase in pension (payable every year in retirement) for each single year that retirement is delayed.

This calculation was made using assumptions valid in early 2009, but the basic principle of pension turbocharging will remain true even if it produces slightly different answers depending on different circumstances at different times. Similarly, the principle will still work (although the precise numbers may be different) whether you are male or female, and whatever retirement ages you are considering.

As you can see from the example, although your circumstances may be different you can usually increase your pension quite substantially by retiring later than you had originally planned.

In fact, the effect could be even greater than the example because we didn't allow for the fact that you might still continue to receive employed income if you retire later. If this happens you have the opportunity to save even more for your pension, making the effect of pension turbocharger even stronger. So by being aware of the huge potential impact of the pension turbocharger and planning your retirement accordingly, you can increase your pension and make a big difference to how the pensions crisis affects you.

While the pension turbocharger can help significantly, it is unlikely to be a full solution to your pension gap, so you should not regard this as a 'get-out clause' to allow you to put off making the maximum provision you can for your retirement as soon as you can.

Conversely, you need to be careful because the pension turbocharger can work against you.

If you choose to retire early in unfavourable circumstances, the combination of factors that make up the pension turbocharger can combine in the opposite direction and cut the value of your pension. Let's look at each factor in turn:

1. Your pension pot is smaller because you and your employer make fewer contributions into your pension.

2. Your pension pot has less time to benefit from investment returns.

3. Because you are retiring earlier, your pension pot will have to stretch over more years of pension payments. So each £1 in the pot buys less pension per year.

4. Your total income falls from your earnings level to the level of your pension, so you have less scope to put money aside for a future pension.

If you have a personal pension or are in a pension scheme and are considering retiring early, you will sometimes see the phrase 'actuarial reduction' used in any calculations that are provided by the pensions administrator. This looks like a huge and arbitrary number, but it is just part of how the pension turbocharger works in reverse. The actuarial reduction refers to the effect of factors 2 and 3 above combined into one number. When this is applied to a pension pot which is already reduced because of factor 1, the numbers can look pretty awful.

Negative turbocharger

Let's look at the 'reverse' of the previous example, which showed that the pension turbocharger had a positive effect. If your pension was due to start at age 65 after 20 years' worth of contributions starting at £1,000 a month, you might retire on a starting pension of £16,200 a year. But if you decided to retire five years early at age 60, the starting pension would fall to roughly £9,200 a year.

In this case the pension turbocharger has worked in reverse and reduced your pension by a whopping 43%, or roughly an 11% reduction for every year that you retire early (annoyingly, although the pension numbers are identical to the previous example, the percentages come out differently depending on whether you are calculating increases or decreases).

As we explained in the previous example, your individual circumstances may be different from these but the effect of the pension turbocharger is likely to be similar.

You can do your own calculation – most of the large insurance companies have a range of useful retirement calculators on their websites. A full list of the tools we refer to are included in the website accompanying this book.

The real-life effect of the pension turbocharger will be even greater than we have illustrated because of the opportunity to earn an income before you retire. If you defer your retirement, you have the opportunity to continue to work and earn extra cash (even if it is a job that pays less than you were used to). Some of this cash could be used to increase your future pension, boosting the positive turbocharger effect.

Conversely, retiring early, particularly from a career job that pays a high salary just before retirement, could lose a lot of cash that could have been used to add to your pension – making the negative turbocharger even more crippling.

So while the old saying 'a bird in the hand is worth two in the bush' applies in many circumstances in life, grabbing the pension bird too soon could easily be a catastrophic move. It's all down to the detail of your own situation, as we will see later.

Summary

- You have a notional share in the money accumulated in every pension plan or scheme that you are part of (except the state pension); we call this your pension pot.

- When you come to retire, your pension pot is effectively used to purchase a pension for the rest of your life. The price of your pension varies depending on your age and health and the type of pension that is purchased.

- Your pension gap is the difference between the amount of pensions you want to retire on, and the amount you actually expect to receive.

- Retiring later can boost your pension by a significant amount because of the pension turbocharger effect. Conversely, retiring early can result in a surprisingly sharp fall in the amount of your pension because the turbocharger also works in reverse.

5

Pensions – under the hood

The variety of options you have and choices you can make to reduce your pension gap, at whatever age, will depend on the type of pension you are considering. This chapter introduces the main types of pension available to you.

Tax relief limits

The main reason to buy a pension as opposed to any other form of investment is the availability of tax relief.

There is no limit on the amount of money you can save in a pension scheme or the number of pension schemes you can save in – although there are limits on the amount of tax relief you can get.

You will get tax relief on contributions up to 100 per cent of your annual earnings. So if you put £1,000 net into your pension scheme, the tax relief the Government gives you on that is worth at least £250. This assumes a basic tax rate of 20%: you make a gross payment of £1,250, the tax relief is worth 20% (i.e. £250), so your net payment is £1,000. If you pay higher rate tax you can claim relief on this – either through PAYE if you are in a company scheme or claiming by entering your pension contributions into your tax returns if you have a personal pension.

There is an annual allowance (for tax relief) of £235,000 in 2008–09 (rising to £255,000 by 2010–11). If your annual pension savings are greater than this, you will be liable to a tax charge on the excess. There is also a limit on the total size of your total pension funds of £1.6 million from 6 April 2007 (rising to £1.8 million by 2010–11 and reviewed thereafter). If your total pension fund is more than this 'lifetime allowance' when you come to take your pension you may be subject to a tax charge.

These allowances are quite high, so most people can save as much as they want towards their retirement without worrying about the tax implications. However, if you think you are likely to come anywhere near the overall lifetime limit you should take independent advice.

Even if you are not a taxpayer you can still get tax relief on pension contributions. You can put in up to £2,880 in any one tax year and the government will top this up with another £720 – giving you total pension savings with tax relief of £3,600 per year.

Once your contributions are inside your pension fund, some taxes are actually payable by the fund but overall it benefits from a lower level of taxation than many other forms of investment – so the growth from interest and investment returns should be greater.

Tax credits

If you are eligible for tax credits (either working tax credit or child tax credit), by making a pension contribution you might be able to increase the amount of tax credit that you receive. This can act like an extra form of tax relief on your pension contributions, making them even more valuable than normal. Unfortunately the rules and mechanics of tax credits are so complicated that we cannot explain them in a book of this nature. If you think you may benefit, you will need to get advice.

For a link to the most up-to-date tax information check our website, **www.thepensionscrisis.com**.

Types of pension

The choices you have, and the decisions you have to make, will vary according to the source of your pension. There are a huge variety of different types of pension and we cannot cover every aspect of all of them in this book. However, there are three broad categories of pension that will determine the actions you take. We introduced them in Chapter 2, and we will continue to refer to them throughout the book.

The three broad types of pension are the following:

1 Final salary pensions (sometimes also described as Defined Benefit pensions)

2 Money purchase pensions (sometimes also described as Defined Contribution pensions)

3 State pension.

It is possible to have slightly different types of pension – for example, based on 'average salary' rather than 'final salary' – but these are still relatively rare so we will concentrate on the main types that people are likely to be involved with.

Final salary pensions

The term 'final salary' refers to a pension scheme which provides a pension that is based on your salary immediately before you retire, irrespective of the level of contributions that you make into the scheme.

The calculation of the pension you will receive has three major elements, which will be defined by the rules of your pension scheme:

1. the number of years' service that counts towards your pension;

2. the 'accrual rate' usually expressed as a fraction, e.g. '1/60th', '1/80th' or '1/100th';

3. the precise definition of your 'final salary' for calculation purposes.

The definition of salary used for calculating your pension varies from scheme to scheme. Often it is not actually your last salary but something like your best year in the last three years – or maybe the average of the last three years, or even the average of the best three years in the last ten. Any bonuses you receive might be treated differently: in some cases they will not be included in the calculation.

Similarly, the number of years' service that count towards your pension will be defined by your employment contract and the scheme rules. There may be a minimum age at which you were allowed to join the scheme, or a minimum length of service before you became a member. In the past it was also common for pension scheme rules to discriminate against female employees. The best thing to do is check your scheme rules or ask the administrators of your pension scheme.

Once these three elements are known, the calculation is fairly straightforward – final salary times qualifying service times the 'accrual rate'. Final salary pension schemes used to be restricted to providing a maximum pension of two-thirds of final salary – so if you are in a '60th' scheme and have 42 years' service, only 40 years may count (whereas in an '80th' scheme all 42 might count if the scheme rules permitted it).

	Scheme 1	Scheme 2
Scheme accrual rate	'80th'	'60th'
Qualifying service	30 years	35 years
Final salary	£30,000	£50,000
Calculation	30,000×30/80	50,000×35/60
Final salary pension	£11,250 a year	£29,167 a year

FIGURE 5.1: How final salary calculations work

Additional voluntary contributions (AVCs)

AVC is the commonly used abbreviation for 'additional voluntary contributions'. Many final salary schemes allow you to pay in extra contributions in order to top up their pension provision. This is a convenient way to add to your pension. Expense charges are generally low (but this is worth checking), you get the advantage of tax relief and your employer manages most of the administration for you via the company's payroll system.

The cash put into an AVC is treated by the scheme as an entirely separate pension pot, held solely for your benefit on top of the normal pensions that the scheme provides. The AVC is accounted for separately and either held within the main pension fund or a separate pension policy.

In effect, most AVC schemes operate like a money purchase pension (see later in this chapter) on top of the scheme benefits, even if the scheme is final salary.

One variant of an AVC is a 'free standing AVC' or FSAVC. These were offered by insurance companies – they are really separate personal pension plans rather than the normal AVC that is offered inside the pension scheme. An FSAVC will normally carry expense charges much like a personal pension – rather than an AVC, where the employer normally meets administration costs – so you need to take this into account. If the expense charges are high, a normal personal pension or stakeholder pension may be better value.

Decline of final salary

As we mentioned previously in Chapter 2, final salary pension schemes have come under a lot of pressure because their costs to employers have risen.

In 1995 there were 5 million private sector employees in final salary schemes that were open to new members. By 2004 this had fallen to 2 million (compared to 7.2 million paying into money purchase schemes). The latest estimate by the Association of Consulting Actuaries (ACA) is that this had fallen to 900,000 by the end of 2007.

Source: 2007 Review and Pensions Trend Survey Report (ACA)

Public sector pension schemes

Public sector pension schemes – those for civil servants, the armed services, politicians and local government employees, and so on – are usually constructed on a final salary basis. In fact, company pension schemes were originally modelled on government pensions, which is why final salary schemes were common. So if you are a member of one of these schemes, everything we have said about final salary schemes applies to you.

Although their benefits operate in a similar way to company final salary schemes, there are two major differences that make them more attractive to members:

1 Usually, public sector pensions are still automatically 'index-linked' – that is, they are increased to reflect increases in the cost of living each year.

2 So far, there has been little attempt to change future benefits in response to the pensions crisis.

Unfunded pensions

The big difference between most public sector schemes and company schemes is that although companies are obliged to set up a pension fund to ensure that members' pensions have some future security, the government does not. As usual, there are exceptions to the rule: for some historical reason local authority pension schemes do have separate pension funds – but pensions for the police, firefighters and teachers are unfunded.

There is no central government pension fund – so current pensions are paid by the government out of general taxation. This means that all future pensions will be paid out of taxes which will be collected in the future. This 'pay-as-you-go' approach obscures the real cost of public sector pensions.

The pensions crisis has had a major impact on company pensions, because when a company agrees to provide a future pension it has to calculate the expected future cost and make appropriate contributions into a fund today. If there is the prospect of a shortfall, the company has to do something about it.

In reality the pensions crisis affects unfunded public sector pensions just as much – but the 'pay-as-you-go' approach makes the problem far less visible today.

The full cost of the pensions crisis on public sector pensions must eventually emerge. When it does, there is likely to be pressure to force public sector pension schemes to cut back – much as has already happened in the private sector. For the time being, a public sector pension is valuable; and even if changes happen in future, these are unlikely to affect any benefits that have already accrued to you if you have one.

> **Key points about 'final salary'**
>
> ❚ *The amount of pension is linked to your final salary, rather than to the contributions you have made.*
>
> ❚ *It is sometimes called 'defined benefit' (DB).*
>
> ❚ *The number of (private) final salary schemes has declined dramatically in recent years.*

Money purchase pensions

We just looked at final salary pensions, where the amount of pension you receive is based on your salary just before retirement and your length of service. By contrast, money purchase pensions put all the contributions (from both you and your employer) into a single cash pot which is invested and builds up until you retire. The cash is then used to buy a pension for you – hence 'money purchase'. These are also referred to as 'defined contribution' (DC) pensions, but we will stick with money purchase because we think the meaning is clearer.

There are two main types of money purchase pensions – personal pensions, and company money purchase schemes.

Personal pension plans

The distinctive thing about a personal pension plan is that it is a pension contract that you take out personally with an authorised pensions product provider – usually an insurance company or an investment company. You are entitled to all the benefits of the relevant policy. The amount it pays out is determined by the policy document itself, not by the government or an employer.

Although this is a fairly simple definition, because of changes in pensions and tax legislation, personal pension plans have acquired a number of different names. For the purposes of this section, personal pension plans include the following:

▌ products officially called 'personal pensions';

▌ self-employed pensions (sometimes known as s226a) – these were the forerunner to personal pensions, initially only available to self-employed people;

▌ buy-out bonds – these are specially designed personal pensions (technically called section 32 contracts), used only when someone leaves a pension scheme. The pension pot for that person can be transferred out of the old pension scheme and transferred into a buy-out bond. In effect, it is a personal pension with only one contribution (the transfer value from the old pension scheme);

▌ self-invested personal pensions (SIPPs) – these are a variant of normal personal pensions, where the policyholder (rather than the insurance company) can directly control how the pension pot is invested (see the description below).

All personal pensions work pretty much in the same way. You pay contributions to the institution you took the policy out with, and they invest the contributions in a pension pot for you. The contributions you make are eligible for tax relief. Every policy will have a different choice of investment funds that it invests in (and you may have the right to choose or switch funds). Every policy will carry its own set of charges deducted from either your contributions or your pension pot to pay for the provider's costs and profits.

Over time, the value inside your personal pension is increased by your contributions and investment growth (hopefully), and reduced by any charges.

SIPPs

Self-invested personal pensions (SIPPs) are a variation on normal personal pensions which allow you to directly control the individual investments that your pension pot purchases (rather than invest in a broader investment fund). At first glance this looks like a very attractive idea, and the schemes have been very popular for small firms buying commercial property (often their own premises) as part of a directors pension scheme. This can be very tax-efficient – though the rules are complex.

Before rushing into such an arrangement, you need to take the following points into account.

▌ Unless you are a skilled investment professional yourself there is a high risk that you will make investment choices that could damage rather than enhance your pension pot. If asked, few people would deliberately gamble their future pensions. Most would prefer a professional investment policy designed for pensions, rather than relying on the good intentions of an amateur. So if you are an amateur, why do it?

▌ SIPPs are more complicated and expensive to manage than mainstream personal pensions. Because of this, the administration charges tend to be higher than normal pensions.

▌ Because they are so complicated, experience suggests that they are more prone to administration errors. If you took out a SIPP, in practice you would be well advised to spend time and energy checking that the administration was being done properly.

Of the 37,000 SIPPs that were sold in the six months from 1 October 2007 to the 31 March 2008, some 25,000 were sold by just the top five providers – demonstrating what a specialist product it is and underscoring the need to obtain independent advice before taking one out.

None of this means that you shouldn't take out a SIPP. If you are highly confident in your own investment expertise (or that of your advisers) and are prepared to pay the extra costs and spend the extra time, then go ahead. But it's a choice that you should only make with your eyes fully open.

Company money purchase schemes

A company money purchase (or DC) scheme is very similar in practice to a personal pension in how it operates. You put money into a pot, and it accumulates as cash.

The technical difference is that the scheme is run and managed by your employer rather than an insurance company. So your pension 'contract' is with the scheme and governed by the scheme rules – you don't have a policy as such. (The scheme may choose to subcontract some of its work to another firm, but this shouldn't affect you.)

In practice, a company money purchase scheme differs from a personal pension in three important ways.

1. Because the scheme has been set up by them, your employers would normally make contributions to your individual pension pot in addition to any contributions that you make. They would normally do this as part of your employment contract with them. In turn, you may also be required to make your own contributions as a condition of the employer making theirs. Any contributions that your employer makes are clearly beneficial because they add to the value of your pension pot.

2 The deductions made from your pension pot to cover the expenses of running the pension are likely to be lower than in a personal pension. This is partly because of economies of scale, and also because a money purchase scheme – unlike a personal pension – does not incur any sales costs in enrolling new members. But the main reason is that employers are not trying to make profits from the pension scheme, and may be prepared to bear some (or all) of the costs of running it. The effect is like having extra contributions into your pot – so you get more pension back at the end.

3 Unlike a personal pension, membership of a company scheme is linked to your employment – so if you leave your job, you have to leave the scheme. All schemes will either refund past contributions or allow the pot to continue to grow, but without further contributions. So if you want to keep building up your pension you will need to make new arrangements for future contributions – and remember to claim your pension from your old employer when you do retire.

Group personal pensions

There is yet another type of money purchase pension that is a half-way house between a personal pension and a standard company money purchase scheme. These are called 'group' personal pensions, and in practice they operate in the same way as normal personal pensions.

The difference is that they are sponsored by an employer: the employer makes all the arrangements with the insurance or investment company rather than you having to do it yourself. The employer would normally (but not necessarily) make a contribution to your policy, and deduct your own contributions from your pay. It's also possible for the expense deductions to be lower because of cost savings to the insurance company.

The benefit to the employer is that they can offer pensions to their staff without having to carry the administration overhead of setting up a scheme. The possible benefits to you are contributions paid by your employer, lower deductions from your policy, and the ability to take your policy with you even if you change jobs.

Stakeholder pensions

As if pensions weren't complicated enough, there are also stakeholder pensions, launched in 2001 by the government. Stakeholder pensions are not state pensions: they are a variation on personal pensions introduced via special legislation. The goal was laudable: to deal with the coming pensions crisis by making a cheap and simple pension plan available to everyone, particularly the less well-off.

In operation, stakeholder pensions are almost identical to personal pensions. They differ only in the maximum expense deductions that can be taken from the pot by the pensions product provider, and the maximum level of contributions that could be made. Originally the contribution limit was £3,600 a year, but this was recently increased to 100% of your salary.

All employers who have more than five full-time employees (or equivalent) and do not have any other pension scheme have to make a stakeholder pension available to their staff. Although they are not obliged to, some employers will also make contributions to your stakeholder pension. If one is available to you, taking out your company's stakeholder pension is definitely worth considering, not least because the deductions from the stakeholder 'pot' are likely to be lower than a normal personal pension.

Unintended consequences

Like many political ideas, stakeholder pensions have suffered from the law of unintended consequences. To try and keep these products as inexpensive as possible, the government placed severe limits on the expenses that could be charged to them. Government limits to contributions also mean that stakeholder pensions are relatively small, so insurance companies couldn't rely on economies of scale to make a profit.

So these are not attractive products for companies to promote. There is certainly not enough profit in stakeholder pensions to justify paying someone to talk them through with you. The result is that most stakeholder pensions have been bought by well-off people who were already pensions aware and paying directly for their pensions advice. Exactly the opposite of the intended market!

You are entitled to take out your own individual stakeholder pension whether or not your employer offers one. Indeed everyone (including children) is entitled to have a stakeholder pension whether or not they are employed. They are not actively promoted by insurance companies (because they can't afford to – see the textbox above on 'unintended consequences'), so you might find them difficult to track down through normal channels. The best bet is government-sponsored information, and our website, **www.thepensionscrisis.com**, has links to the relevant sites.

Key points about 'money purchase'

▌ *The amount of pension is linked to the contributions you have made plus any contributions your employer has made on your behalf. There is no direct link with the level of your salary.*

▌ *It is sometimes called 'defined contribution' (DC).*

▌ *All personal pensions are money purchase, and more and more company pension schemes are switching to money purchase because the contribution levels are lower and more controllable.*

State pensions

State pensions have been in existence in the UK since 1908 when Lloyd George, the Chancellor of the Exchequer at the time, introduced them. At first they were aimed primarily at the poor and were means-tested; that is to say an individual had to prove a low level of income to qualify. Since then they have become available to everybody of retirement age. As part of the welfare state along with the national health service, free education, unemployment payments and other social benefits, many people have come to expect the state pension to be sufficient money for them to retire on.

Sadly, this is an unfounded expectation. As we saw in Chapter 3 (Myth 2: I can live on the basic state pension), those who have not made additional provision or do not have caring relatives, will find themselves barely able to survive on the state pension.

Basic state pension

Most of us are entitled to the basic state pension. Unlike other forms of pension, there is no separate fund which is built up over time. State pensions are paid out of general taxation and are often described as 'pay-as-you-go' because there is no fund. All the money you have paid into your national insurance scheme has already been spent on those being paid a pension at the time; it has not been stored away and invested on your behalf.

The level of the basic state pension is set annually by the Chancellor. In recent years it has been linked to the overall level of price inflation (not wage inflation, which tends to be higher).

At £90.70 a week for a single person the basics state pension is not huge, but according to Age Concern 63% of pensioners receive at least half their income from state pensions and benefits.

When it is paid

Historically, the basic state pension has been paid starting at age 65 for men and 60 for women, but there have been a couple of changes in recent years.

First, a combination of rising costs and the requirement to avoid sex discrimination means that the retirement age is being harmonised over time to age 65 for both men and women – then later to age 68.

Second, a new choice has been introduced: if you decide to defer your pension, the amount you receive, at your later retirement, will be increased.

Chapter 8, 'At the point of retirement', provides more detail about state pensions and how to work out your state retirement age. More comprehensive information can be obtained from the links on our website.

Earnings-related state pensions

You may be entitled to an additional state pension (also called the State Second Pension and formerly the State Earnings Related Pension Scheme (SERPS)). As its name suggests, additional state pension is paid in addition to the basic state pension.

These additional pensions are so complicated and confusing that there is little point attempting to explain them fully here. Any statements you receive from the government will contain numbers that are relevant to you specifically – this is the information that you really need.

If you do want to understand in greater detail how these numbers are calculated, full information is available on government websites which can be accessed directly from **www.thepensionscrisis.com**.

Pension Credit

Pension Credit is a state benefit rather than a state pension, but it is interwoven with the way that state pension works.

If you are over age 60 and have a total income of less than £124.05 per week if you are single (£189.35 if you have a partner), the Pension Credit will guarantee that you receive at least these amounts.

So at first glance it might look as if it is simply raising the minimum level of state pension that everyone receives – until you spot the trap.

> If a man aged 65 is entitled to the basic state pension and has no savings or pension or other income, he may receive a Pension Credit of £33.35 a week. In current market conditions, you would need a pension pot of £39,000 to buy this amount of pension.
>
> If the same person has £25,000 in a bank account, he gets £17.85 a week in Pension Credit – a drop of £15.90. The 'lost' pension is worth over £18,500.
>
> If he has £50,000 in a bank account he gets no Pension Credit at all, so loses the full value of £39,000.
>
> Source: Pension Service Pension Credit calculator, and currently available pension annuity rates.

The trap is that if you have any other pension or savings, you lose your entitlement to Pension Credit on a '£1 for £1' basis. So if you are expecting to retire on or below the Pension Credit level of income, you might wish to avoid saving, or spend any savings that you do have.

If you are over age 65, you can get 'Savings Credit' so that you are not penalised as much for having savings. In effect this makes sure you get at least 60p for every £1 you have saved – an improvement but still poor value for money (and terribly complicated to calculate and understand).

Two more bits of bad news. If you have cash savings of over £6,000 these are deemed to provide annual income at a high rate of £100 for every £1,000 in savings – so in current conditions you could lose far more than £1 for every £1 saved. And if your savings take your income above Pension Credit level, you lose any chance of entitlement to Housing Benefit and/or Council Tax Benefit.

You can get a quotation for how much Pension Credit you might receive from the Pensions Service website – a link is available at **www.thepensionscrisis.com**.

State pension: key points

▌ *The amount of the basic state pension is fixed by government and usually increases each year in line with price inflation.*

▌ *The additional state earnings-related pension (SERPS) depends on what you have earned (within limits) during your working life.*

▌ *You have limited choices about how or when you receive your state pension.*

Of course, pensions are not the only potential source of retirement income. They are the most efficient though, because they have been specifically designed for the purpose and are usually boosted by tax relief on both contributions and investment returns.

Later on, particularly in Chapter 7, we will explore other options for using your financial assets to generate an income in retirement.

Summary

▌ There are three main types of pension – final salary pensions, money purchase pensions and state pensions.

▌ Final salary schemes pay a pension equal to a proportion of your salary before retirement, irrespective of what contributions were made.

▌ Company pension schemes can either be final salary or money purchase.

▌ Public sector pension schemes are usually final salary, and are still the most generous type of final salary scheme.

▌ Money purchase schemes use the money you and your employer have contributed to buy a pension at retirement. All personal pension plans are money purchase.

▌ Within the broad headings of final salary and money purchase, there are many different types of pension.

▌ The state pension scheme has two components – the basic state pension and an additional earnings-related pension.

Understanding your pension gap

Before investing a huge amount of time and effort in tackling your pensions crisis, you might want to work out how big your own pension gap is. For most people, doing a very rough calculation is probably sufficient to get an idea of the scale of the gap and therefore the scale of the action that needs to be taken.

Your pension gap

To start thinking about the actions you might want to take, it's useful to get a rough idea of the size of your pension gap. Conceptually this is a fairly easy calculation:

1 work out what you will need in retirement;

2 work out how much you will actually get from all the available sources;

3 calculate the difference.

In practice, the calculation can get very messy – and a full detailed analysis is unlikely to be feasible for most people. As we said though, all you need is a rough idea.

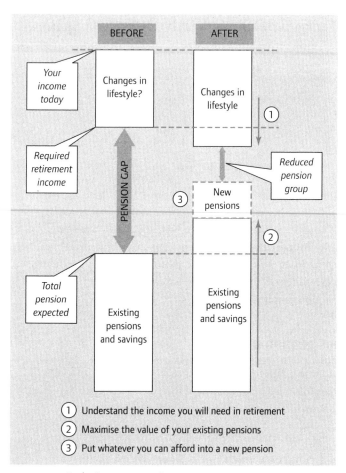

FIGURE 6.1: Reducing your pension gap

We will now walk you through the full calculation of your pension gap. Once again, the point is not to try and be 100% accurate because that is almost impossible: what you really need is an idea of the scale of the potential problem.

How much you will need when you retire

Changes when you retire

You are currently spending money to support your lifestyle today, so that is a solid starting point. Having understood that, you can then make adjustments to allow for the changes in lifestyle and spending patterns that you expect to happen when you retire.

So start by constructing a simple list of how you spend your money today, for example:

▌ Mortgage

▌ Food and clothing

▌ Utilities

▌ Entertainment

▌ Travel.

Then work out which ones will change when you retire. An obvious example is that most mortgages are designed to stop before retirement, so hopefully that can be completely omitted from your calculation. You will not have to spend on travelling to and from work, but you may expect to travel more to visit friends and family.

There are a couple of less obvious categories. The first is spending which is driven by your income level rather than by your genuine lifestyle needs. You could describe these as luxuries rather than necessities, maybe things like expensive restaurants or even works of art. We may add some of these back later on, but for now keep them out of the calculation so that you know the basic amount of income you will actually need.

The second is your housing costs. Even if your mortgage is paid off utility bills can be very high. If you are not working you may spend more time at home, and the cost of heating a large house has risen enormously in recent years.

Trialling

While working out sums and calculation on paper looks sensible, it is difficult to get a good 'feel' for whether the results are realistic or not.

One way to cut through this is to test out how comfortable it would be to live on your estimated post-retirement income, by actually doing it for a period. Obviously you can't really stop your mortgage payments, but you can make a conscious decision to work within most of the other elements of your income and just see how it works out.

Extra costs

You also need to factor in the likely cost of the extra things you will be doing after you retire.

At a basic level you will have more free time to do all the things you should have been doing while you were working – home repairs, DIY, gardening and whatever else. All of these will have costs attached.

But retirement is about more than basics; it's an opportunity to do lots of the nice things that you didn't have time to do while working – maybe extra holidays, theatre trips, and so on. You need to build the likely cost of these things into your post-retirement budget, along with some of the other luxury items that we removed earlier.

Healthcare

One of the major post-retirement costs that is very easy to overlook is healthcare. Most of us have had reasonable health throughout our working lives and the NHS has been available if something goes wrong. Even if we have had private healthcare in the past, this is often viewed as a luxury rather than a necessity. We are simply not used to having to worry about the cost of healthcare.

But things are different in retirement. The NHS is well placed to provide support for short-term health issues like accidents and illnesses (known in the health world as 'acute care'). But it is no longer able to cope with the long-term care (also known as 'chronic care') that is often required by people in the ever-growing retired population.

If you do nothing and eventually find yourself needing long-term care, local authorities have the right to seize some of your assets to pay for your care. And as we saw in Chapter 2 the costs are potentially high – between £25,000 and £35,000 a year. Clearly, this has the potential to ruin all sorts of careful financial planning around retirement and inheritance, so it is worth taking into account.

There are a number of different actions you can take in advance to prepare for this possibility, from buying a special insurance policy to transferring assets – or simply accepting the risk. The subject of long-term care is so large and complex that it deserves a book by itself. All we can do here is alert you to the fact that it is something you need to think about.

Further information can be obtained from our website, **www.thepensioncrisis.com**. If you want to take action in this area, we recommend that you get some expert advice (see Chapter 12).

Means-testing for long-term care

Care costs are broken down into three components: accommodation, personal care and nursing care. The NHS will automatically make a contribution for the cost of nursing care. In Scotland (but not the rest of the UK), the state also pays for the cost of personal care. In the rest of the UK you are personally liable for the cost of accommodation and personal care, subject to a means test.

The Community Care Act 1991 formalised means testing, which means that if care is needed, two tests will be carried out. The first is a test of actual care needs (known as a section 47 care assessment), the second is a test of means. Crudely, if you have assets exceeding about £22,000 (the amounts vary throughout the UK), local authority financial assistance is not available. Below that level, a complicated sliding-scale formula is applied.

If you attempt to take actions designed to benefit from means testing (like giving your assets away or spending all your money), the amount involved will be added back to the amount of assets used in the means test calculation.

Links to more detailed information are available on our website.

How much you will get when you retire

State pensions

A good starting point, because almost everyone who has ever paid National Insurance contributions receives it, is the state pension.

As we described in Chapter 5, the state pension has two main components – basic state pension and additional state pension (including SERPS).

You can get a full personal statement of how much state pension you are likely to receive from the Pensions Service by applying through their website (a link to this is available at our website, **www.pensionscrisis.com**).

SERPS

'SERPS' stands for 'state earnings-related pension'.

SERPS is a scheme that provided an extra state pension on top of the basic state pension. You automatically contributed to SERPS if the period you were employed ran from 6 April 1978 to 5 April 2002. After that, the scheme was slightly modified and renamed the 'State Second Pension' (or 'additional State Pension' just to make things even clearer!)

Your state pension forecast will include all the basic state pension and additional state pension that you are entitled to, including any from the old Graduated Retirement Benefit scheme that operated between 1961 and 1975.

Much more information, including details of how these pensions can be inherited by relatives, is available on the Pensions Service website (see the link at **www.thepensionscrisis.com**).

Contracted-out SERPS

When the SERPS scheme was running, there was a facility to 'contract-out' of the SERPS scheme. Basically this meant that instead of paying all of your National Insurance contributions to the government, you could elect for the equivalent amount of part of your NI contributions to be paid either into your company pension scheme or a personal pension.

This was an attractive option for many people, particularly at younger ages, because the prospects for investment growth made it likely that you could get a higher pension than the government was offering. In many cases, contracting-out became the default choice.

If you were contracted-out for a period, by definition you will not see a SERPS pension on the government pension forecast. However, you should see an equivalent SERPS pension for the same period included in the statements you receive from your company pension scheme or personal pension. SERPS pensions are always identified separately on statements because of their special status.

Contracting back in

The ways the SERPS numbers worked, it was often attractive for younger people with money purchase pensions to 'contract-out' of SERPS (or the state second pension) because investment returns over a long period could outstrip the benefits the government was offering. This was not generally the case for older people. For the same reason if you did contract out many years ago, you will ultimately reach an age when you are likely to do better if you 'contract back in' to the SERPS state pension scheme.

(To be clear, none of this applies to contracted-out final salary schemes, because benefits here are defined by scheme rules rather than dependent on the investment performance of your pension.)

The switch-over age isn't fixed – it varies each year with circumstances, but is likely to be somewhere in your 50s. In most cases pension scheme administrators and personal pension companies will write to the people concerned when the timing is right. If you want to check for yourself, our website **www.thepensionscrisis.com** *has links to the latest information.*

Pensions from your employers

The next place to start gathering information is from the pension scheme of your current and past employers.

Your current employer should be the easiest: simply ask them for a statement of your future projected pensions from the scheme (you may already have one in your records).

This will be actually provided by the pension scheme administrators, but you can start by asking the HR or Personnel department.

Past employers are slightly more tricky, particularly if you have lost contact with them. Bear in mind that even if they had a pension scheme, you may not have any remaining entitlement to a pension at all. Each scheme is governed by its own rules and these cover exactly how and when pension entitlements are triggered. The most likely reasons that you may not have a remaining pension are:

▌ You were too young to join the scheme.

▌ You didn't stay with the employer for the qualifying period.

▌ You took a return of all your contributions in exchange for any pension rights when you left employment.

▌ You transferred your pension rights out of that scheme, either to a new employers' scheme or to a personal pension policy that you own.

It is easy to forget exactly what happened, so the best thing to do is write to the latest addresses of all the employers you have worked for in the past, and ask them. We have provided a sample letter on our website, **www.thepensionscrisis.com**. In addition there are links to several resources on-line to help you trace missing pensions. These include the following:

▌ the pensions tracing service, which can be accessed from the Department of Work and Pensions website;

▌ the pensions regulator, who has a database of all company pension schemes going back to 1975 and may be able to help trace companies going back before that;

▌ the unclaimed assets register (run by Experian, the credit rating agency) which will trace any unclaimed assets, pensions, life policies, etc. on your behalf – for a fee.

Personal pensions

As we mentioned earlier, personal pensions are the type where you have your own policy directly with an insurance (or investment) company.

You should have been getting statements about how your policy is doing, and what pension you might expect, every year. If you have lost contact with the insurance company (or have lost your latest statement), simply write to them using the sample letter on our website, **www.thepensionscrisis.com**. Even if you stopped making contributions a long time ago, your policy is still likely to have some value (the technical term is a 'paid-up' value).

Many insurance companies have been taken over in recent years. When this happens, your policy is still safe and secure (because the regulations are so tight), but you might find it difficult to track down the company who is now responsible for it. Once again, there are several links on our website that can help you with this.

Apples and pears

Once you have collected all the data about your state pension entitlement, and how much you will get from current and past company schemes and from personal pensions, you can then work out the total pension you will receive.

But first, you need to make sure that you don't mix up apples and pears. When you add numbers together, they need to be consistent with each other.

The first thing to watch out for is the difference between 'real' numbers and cash numbers.

Add pension to pension

On any statement you receive from a pension scheme or personal pension, there are two distinct types of numbers. First, there are pension amounts – the amounts which will be paid to you every year in retirement. On the same page you will often see references to cash sums too, and it is crucial that you don't confuse these. A cash sum is a lump sum, a fixed amount (like the cash in your bank account) that you get only once, whereas a pension amount is payable to you on a regular basis.

Pension statements have to mention cash sums when they talk about:

▌ the total size of your pension pot for money purchase schemes and personal pensions;

▌ a 'transfer value': if you left this pension scheme and opted to transfer into a new personal pension, this is the amount of cash that would be transferred into your new policy to become the pension pot in the new policy. (The transfer value is often lower than the full pension pot in the old pension because the company applies a penalty if the money is taken away.);

▌ a 'tax-free cash' amount. One of the options you have on retirement (see Chapter 8) is to take a lower pension and receive a tax-free cash sum instead.

So make sure the numbers you are looking at for this purpose are all pension amounts, not cash sums.

Cash obstacles

To be completely consistent, you should make sure that you look at the pension amount *before* it has been reduced to make provision for tax-free cash. Some pension schemes, mainly government and local authority schemes, make this difficult because the tax-free cash is provided separately rather than by reducing the pension amount. If the tax-free cash is small this will not be a problem, but if it is large you could convert it into an equivalent pension amount using a rough conversion rate. (See the link to open market option rates on our website, **www.thepensionscrisis.com**.)

Inflation and 'real' numbers

If you get a personal forecast from the government website it will be in 'today's money values'. In other pension forecasts you might receive, you will sometimes see the phrase 'in real terms'. Both are intended to mean the same thing.

The idea is to cancel out the effect of inflation on the cash numbers you are looking at by converting them into today's purchasing power. So, for example, a pension of £20,000 starting in 20 years' time might only be worth £10,000 in today's purchasing power (on the assumption that the cost of living has doubled over that period). So the 'real' equivalent of the £20,000 yearly pension is £10,000.

A couple of things to bear in mind. First, inflation is a complex subject and no one can predict accurately how much it will be, or exactly which items will increase in price the fastest. So it can only be an estimate (even for the government, which usually links state pensions to a price inflation index).

Second, even if as in the example the 'real' pension is quoted as £10,000, that's not how much you would actually get – you would still get the £20,000. (And conversely, if you wanted to make sure that you could afford £10,000-worth of goods in future, you would need to build up a pension of £20,000.)

Retirement age

The next thing to be consistent about is retirement age. The state pension has a fixed retirement age for you, which will be declared on your state pension forecast. (As we described in Chapter 5, the pensions crisis is forcing changes in state retirement age in future, but the one given to you will stay the same.)

You have a lot more flexibility about retirement age in other types of pension. For example, it is common for company pensions to start at age 60 and for personal pensions to permit retirement at any age beyond 50 (although this is increasing to 55 soon – see Chapter 8). There is a universal rule that all pensions must commence before age 75.

For consistency, it is therefore best to start with the state retirement age when looking at all your pensions. Most of the statements you get will automatically include this, but if not you can ask for the extra information.

Escalation and other options

One of the options you have when you take your pension is the 'escalation rate' – how much it increases each year after you retire. We will explore the escalation rate in greater detail later in Chapter 7 when we look at the options you will have when you retire.

For now, since the state pension is inflation-proofed, for comparison we should start with inflation-proofed pensions. Many statements will already have this information available and, once again, you can always ask for it.

There are other possible pensions options which are discussed in Chapter 8, and we could go on for a long time trying to be consistent in every detail. If you are of a technical mind, that would be a sensible thing to do. But for most people, making sure we are talking using 'real' numbers, a common retirement age and the same escalation is sufficient to have a solid starting point for decision-making.

Other adjustments

To complete the picture, you might want to think about other state benefits that are available to you on retirement. For most people these benefits are likely to be pretty small – so you may decide to skip this step.

Your entitlements may include Winter Fuel payment, Pension Credit benefit, and Council Tax and Housing benefits. Links to information about the current level of benefits are available at our website, **www.thepensionscrisis.com**.

Bringing it all together

Your pension gap is simply the difference between how much you will get and how much you will need. And if you really want to depress yourself, you can convert your pension gap into cash terms by using one of the conversion factors described in Chapter 8!

The object of this exercise is not to be precise, but:

▌ to establish whether the pensions crisis has affected you;

▌ to find out the rough size of your pension gap so that your mind can focus on how much you need to be concerned.

Unless you have been in a government or generous final salary pension scheme for most of your career, you are likely to find out that you do have a gap, and need to start thinking positively about how you can reduce it.

You can take the first action right now. When you calculated how much you will need in retirement, if you are like most people you probably erred on the generous side in terms of wanting to maintain a top-notch lifestyle. Now is the time to 'loop back' to that section and make a more realistic assessment. The rest of this book is devoted to other actions you can take to reduce your pension gap.

Summary

❚ How detailed an approach you take in calculating your pension gap depends on your own style and preferences.

❚ Your pension gap is the difference between two things:

  1 the amount of pension you think you will need to live reasonably comfortably in retirement;

  2 the amount of pension, from all the different possible sources, that you are likely to get.

❚ There are a range of resources available to support you in tracing your pension policies.

❚ You need to be consistent in how you deal with various aspects of your pension so that you are comparing like with like, and get an accurate idea of your likely income.

❚ It is very likely that you have a pension gap. The important thing is not to panic; just focus on what action you can take.

3

A practical toolkit

In this section we outline some typical issues and options relating to each life stage, together with tips and suggestions about what you can do to start closing your own pension gap. You will want to focus on your present life stage first, but you will also find it illuminating to understand the options available at other stages – particularly if you haven't got there yet.

Already retired

I f you have already retired, you might be fortunate because you 'ducked' the pensions crisis before it hit – or it might be staring you right in the face. Either way, there are still things you can think about to improve your situation. These are also useful pointers to keep in your back pocket if you are thinking about retiring in the not-too-distant future.

Getting what you are entitled to

The first thing to do is to check that you have tapped into all the available sources of income and benefits. This may seem obvious, but the field is so complicated that it is very easy to overlook a potential source of income. Here are some of the places to look.

▌ The pension schemes of all the employers you worked for, whether or not you believe you are entitled to pension benefits. The trustees of company pension schemes have the discretion to change the level of benefits, even to past members, so it is worthwhile checking with them. The text of a sample letter to these pension schemes can be downloaded from our website.

▌ Pension policies and other policies (like endowments) that you thought you once had. Even if you stopped paying premiums or contributions a long time ago, many policies still have a value (called a 'paid-up' value) that you are entitled to receive. If you moved house, the insurance company would not have been able to contact you to make payment. Most insurance companies have an embarrassingly large number of these 'paid-up' policies where they have lost contact with the customer. There are several tracing services available on-line which can help. See our website for details.

The text of a sample letter to insurance companies can be downloaded from our website. The same letter can also be used to track down 'lost' bank and building society accounts and other products like PEPs and TESSAs.

▌ State benefits, either benefits that everyone is entitled to (like winter fuel payment) or those which are means-tested. A list of state benefits is contained in the pension gap calculation in Chapter 6, and current values can be obtained via our website.

Getting a good deal on things you use regularly

It is always worth checking that you are getting the best deal available on services you use regularly. For example, utility bills, phone and TV charges, all insurances, credit cards and savings accounts. A few minutes spent checking you are on the best rate could prove to be very beneficial.

If you are over 60 you may be able to get a grant to insulate and draught-proof your home, which could help reduce your heating bills. You can learn more from the website of the Energy Saving Trust.

You may also be able to get help installing central heating. For more information get a copy of Help the Aged's guide 'Keep out the cold' which gives advice on saving energy.

Find out if you can save money by switching or combining your utility providers, for example gas and electricity. You can also spread the cost by using direct debits. Compare the cost of gas and electricity offered by different companies on the Energywatch website.

Price comparison websites (such as Moneysupermarket.com) can be very useful in helping you to review your phone package, various insurances, and other financial products.

Links to all the above are available on our website.

Claim what you are entitled to

While it is clear that you cannot rely on the state pension alone to provide for you in retirement, there are other benefits available – particularly Pension Credit (see Chapter 5). If you are already retired you should ensure you claim all the benefits that you are entitled to. The DWP estimates that nearly £5 billion of means-related benefits that should go to older people remain unclaimed each year. There have been several campaigns to raise the profile of this issue and understand why people are not claiming.

The reasons for not claiming seem to be a mix of pride and complexity. The taxman has never been embarrassed about taking a significant part of your income in the past and few of us are happy being forced to pay, so it seems perverse not to take the opportunity to claim some of it back if you are legally entitled to do so. There is no doubt that complexity is a barrier, but these days there is a lot of information and support available – you just need to be a bit persistent. Our website has links to sources of useful information.

Getting value from your house

Using your house

Not surprisingly, for most people the house that they live in is their single biggest (non-pension) asset. In theory, you could convert this into cash. In practice it's more complicated because if you simply sell up, you incur the costs of doing so and will have to move out and find somewhere else to live.

There are other ways of using some of the equity in your house to generate income, and these are covered next.

Equity release schemes

Over the past few years, equity release schemes have been developed as a new way of tapping into the value of your home. They seem to offer a natural way of connecting historically high property values with the growing need for extra cash in retirement.

The main attraction of equity release schemes is that they offer to give you cash now in exchange for losing some of the equity in your property at a future date. That can be helpful either if you just need some cash, or want to eliminate consumer debts that have a high interest rate. A key point is that you don't have to move out of your home in order to get the extra money.

The main disadvantages of equity release schemes are the following:

▌ they can be complex and difficult to understand;

▌ administration charges (often difficult to see because of the complexity) can be high, particularly if small amounts of money are being raised;

▌ depending on the structure of the scheme, you could lose a lot more of the equity in your house than you expected;

▌ children often build an expectation that they will inherit the house when you pass away: the value of this inheritance could be severely reduced.

There are two main types of equity release scheme – home reversions and lifetime mortgages.

Home reversions

With a home reversion scheme, you effectively sell a proportion of your house now for cash but are allowed to live in it until you die. So for a house valued at £300,000 you might sell one-third of it. But you don't get £100,000 for this because the company that gives you cash today probably has to wait a long time until it gets repaid (you may only get £60,000, for example). When you do pass away, the house might be sold for, say, £450,000. Of this, one-third – £150,000 – goes to repay the home reversion company and £300,000 goes to your estate.

The big advantage of a home reversion plan is that you always retain a fixed proportion of the value of your property. You receive cash tax-free, and don't have to make any repayments.

The big disadvantage of a home reversion plan is that you are giving up the possibility of increases in property values on the proportion of the house that you effectively sell. You are also selling at a discount in exchange for not paying rent, so if you happen to pass away early your estate makes a net loss.

Lifetime mortgages

With a lifetime mortgage, you simply take out a mortgage for a percentage of the value of your house. There are two main differences between a lifetime mortgage and the normal mortgage that we are all familiar with.

1. There is no fixed term – the mortgage continues until you die.

2. You don't have to make interest or capital repayments until you die or move house. Interest is still charged at a commercial rate and builds up on the value of your outstanding mortgage.

For a house valued at £300,000 you might, for example, take a mortgage of £50,000. Over the years, interest will be added to your outstanding mortgage. The amount repaid when you pass away could easily, for example, build to £100,000 or more.

The big advantage of a lifetime mortgage is that you retain all the potential future growth in property values on your house (less the interest due on the loan) in exchange for tax-free cash. If you die early, your estate only has to cover a small amount of interest on top of the mortgage repayment.

Equally, the big disadvantage of a lifetime mortgage is that you are taking the full risk on property prices. If you have a large mortgage and interest rates outstrip increases in property values, the value of your house could be completely wiped out by the time you die (although most plans guarantee that the value will never go negative).

There is a variation on a lifetime mortgages called a 'drawdown lifetime mortgage'. This means that after the mortgage is approved, you only have to take as much cash as you need, when you need it. This has the obvious advantage that you can keep the outstanding mortgage (and therefore interest payments) as low as possible. However, you should expect to have to pay a slightly higher interest rate for this extra flexibility.

A fuller description of the types of equity release scheme available and the things to watch out for are beyond the scope of this book – links to more comprehensive information are available on our website.

Equity release schemes are a useful additional tool for people who are struggling to cope with the pensions crisis. However, note the following points.

1 The schemes are inherently costly to put together because of their complexity. Because of this, you should exhaust all other avenues for generating the money that you need before taking out an equity release scheme.

2 If you do decide to go ahead, you must get professional advice. Elsewhere in this book, we have often referred to the desirability of obtaining professional advice: in this case we do think it is a 'must'.

Financial Services Authority (FSA) advice

Equity release schemes can be helpful but they are not suitable for everyone. You may consider these alternatives if you need money:

- *selling your current home and buying a smaller property – you'd keep full ownership of your new home and avoid paying interest on a loan;*

- *contacting your local council or other organisation to check if you could claim money to pay for home repairs or improvements;*

- *claiming any state benefits you may be entitled to;*

- *tracing any private pensions or investments that you may have lost track of;*

- *using your savings or selling any investments – but consider getting advice before doing so.*

Downsizing

By far the most economic way to extract value from the equity in your house is to sell and move to somewhere smaller and less expensive. By doing this, you will receive cash without any of the costs and strings attached to some form of 'equity release' scheme. Naturally there are costs involved in selling and moving, but these are easily quantified and can be taken into account when making a decision.

There are two big advantages in downsizing over equity release. First, it is a simple transaction that you are probably familiar with and provides absolute certainty about where you stand – there are no concerns about what might happen in the future and the situation is clear and open to your next of kin. Second, although moving house has costs, so do equity release plans. There is a real danger that they could be high compared to the amount of money that is actually being released.

The obvious disadvantage of downsizing is that you will be living in a less expensive house. But if you can't afford to live on your current pension while living in a more expensive house, it's probably better to face up to the realities of the situation and deal with it cleanly. Having gone through the obvious disruption of moving house, you may even find somewhere that is far more suitable to your needs in retirement than your previous home.

An alternative to downsizing which has many of its advantages is to consider renting out a room or two in your existing house – if it is sufficiently large. This could provide a useful additional income in retirement – and you don't have to go through the cost and disruption of moving house.

Costs of equity release

The terms of each type of equity release plan are slightly different, so there are no standard costs. However, you should expect to pay between 5% and 6% of the mortgage amount, plus an arrangement fee (maybe £500) and legal fees.

By comparison, downsizing (i.e. moving house) might cost you about 1.5% for the estate agent plus stamp duty (varying from 0% to 4% depending on value) plus legal fees and the actual cost of moving.

Joint ownership

A variation of the 'downsizing' option that some families consider is for the retired person or couple to sell their home and live with the next generation – either in the existing home or a larger one funded by the sale of both existing homes.

This has a number of clear economic advantages. First, the 'cost per person' of living in the enlarged home could be lower than living separately – and the retired person may be able to retain some of their cash from the house sale to boost their income. If the next generation also owns the new home completely, this could also be quite efficient from the point of view of inheritance tax and the risk of having to pay for long-term care (as long as it isn't done solely for this purpose).

Of course, such a move has personal implications that are stronger than simple economics issues, and these are likely to be the most important criteria when making such a big decision. What will the relationships between the generations be like in such a radically different environment? What impact would such a 'deal' have on other family members, particularly siblings of the younger generation?

Assets versus income

As we saw in Chapter 4, every pension has a 'price' in terms of how much cash you need to purchase it. The same concept also applies to financial assets that you don't hold inside a pension: if you want to convert these assets into income you need to think in terms of a price. And, as with pensions, the price is probably higher than you suspect.

Many people think of the equity in their houses as being their largest asset, and one that they can easily use to fund their retirement. For example, let's just assume that you believe that you have £100,000 of equity in your house that you could easily release using one of the methods described earlier in this chapter. If your pension price is 25 (using the same number as in the example in Chapter 4), this would buy you an income of only £4,000 a year for life. Probably less than you expected.

Naturally your actual price will vary according to your own circumstances and current prices in the market, but you get the point. You need a lot of assets to buy any sort of worthwhile income, and you probably can't rely on the equity in your house alone to provide a comfortable retirement.

Converting assets into income

So far we have been hunting down all the possible sources of income available to you, but you may also be able to add to this by converting some of your assets into extra income. 'Income' is defined as money you expect to receive from year to year, whereas 'assets' are things that you own. Assets can be either tangible items like jewellery or works of art, or financial contracts like bank accounts, stocks and shares and savings policies. For the purpose of this section the assets we are interested in are those that can be turned into cash.

Once you convert your assets into cash, you can then use the cash to buy additional income. This can be done in different ways.

'Do-it-yourself'

The simplest, but also the most risky, way to generate income from assets is to guess how many years you think you are likely to live and divide the cash into equal instalments. If the cash is invested in a bank account, it will earn interest and this can be used to top up your income each year.

The major problem with this approach is that you are extremely unlikely to guess the date of your death correctly, even if you wanted to try! If you die sooner than you expected there will be cash left over – which may be fine for your estate but not very efficient for you. Worse, if you live longer than you expected your cash will simply run out. Trying to do it yourself, which is a bit of a lottery, is even more complicated if two of you need to receive income from the same source.

Because of the high risks involved, this is not an attractive option. The one exception might be if you are in desperately poor health and are only expected to live a short time – in these circumstances you may be able to plan your finances accordingly. But even here you need to think about making proper provision for your spouse if he or she is expected to live a reasonably long time.

More efficient approaches

We will describe three ways of using assets more efficiently than a 'do-it-yourself' approach:

1. Buy an annuity
2. 'Drawdown'
3. Live off your assets.

Buying an annuity

An 'annuity' is a financial product sold by life insurance companies that, in exchange for a cash lump sum, produces an annual income until you die. The insurance company is taking a gamble on how long you will live, but can afford to do so because it is averaging the risk out over thousands of different people.

The big advantage of an annuity is that it removes any guessing or worry about how long you will live. The insurance company is taking that risk, based on its assessment of your average life expectancy.

Pension annuities and purchased life annuities

Money purchase pension schemes and personal pension plans have to buy annuities. This is because when you decide to retire, the cash that was held in your pension pot has to be converted into an annual pension, and buying an annuity is the most effective way to do this – hence the name money purchase. As we will see later on, in Chapter 8, you can influence this transaction to your own benefit by exercising your open market option (OMO). Annuities bought by a pension are called 'pension annuities'.

Differences in pension and life annuities

The main difference between pension and purchased life annuities is the way they are treated in your tax returns. The full income from a pension must be declared on your tax returns (this is reasonably fair because you already received tax relief while your pension was building up).

The income from a purchased life annuity that you buy using your own cash (which you have already paid tax on) is treated more favourably for tax. A proportion of every income payment you receive is treated by the taxman as a return of the cash that you originally paid for the annuity – so is not taxable. You only need to pay tax on the element that is 'deemed' to have been generated by investment returns. Fortunately, you don't have to work this out for yourself: the insurance company that you bought the annuity from will tell you how much you need to declare.

The other difference, which works in the other direction, is that the cost of buying a purchased life annuity is slightly higher than the cost of a comparable pension annuity.

Partly, this is because there are a lot more people who are buying annuities with pension fund money than with other cash, so the market is bigger and more competitive. But also, life companies think they are taking more risk when they sell life annuities. If you have your own cash and you are in extremely poor health you would do better to keep the cash than buy an annuity – so purchased life annuities only tend to get purchased by people in good health. They will live longer on average, and the rates are higher to reflect this. With a pension fund you have to buy an annuity eventually, whatever your state of health.

You can also buy an annuity with your own cash, whether or not you have a pension. When you do this, technically you are buying a 'purchased life annuity'. Pension annuities and purchased life annuities are very similar: it's just that one is purchased by a pension while the other is bought with your own cash (although there are different tax treatments – see the textbox above). Throughout this book, when we refer to annuity rates we will always use pension annuity rates for consistency.

Factors affecting your life expectancy

If you are in good health, age is the dominant determinant of your life expectancy, followed by whether you are male or female. Females have higher life expectancy than males in all countries.

Life expectancy differs from population to population. For example in the UK, life expectancy is highest in England and lowest in

Scotland. For both men and women, there is a social gradient such that those in the unskilled manual class have the lowest life expectancy and those in the professional class the highest.

Providers of annuities generally take your age and gender into account and, in some cases, your state of health. Recently, social factors (like where you live) have also started to be taken into account, by varying prices according to your postcode.

The amount of annuity income that you can receive depends on your age, your sex, your state of health and the way that you want income payments to be structured for the remainder of your life. Let's start by looking at how the amount of annuity you receive is greater if you are a man (because men live less long than women), and greater the older you are (because you have a shorter time to live).

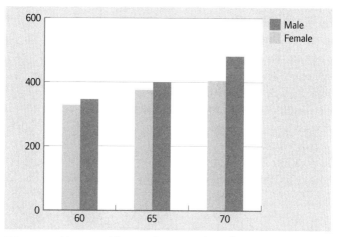

FIGURE 7.1: How annuities vary by age and gender
Monthly income for £100,000 invested. Single life, 3% escalation, guaranteed 5 years.

Swings and roundabouts

Another way to think about an annuity is that it is the
opposite of a savings account. A savings account (or
endowment policy) is a product where you invest money
over a period of time and receive a cash sum at the end. You
accumulate your cash over time.

By contrast, an annuity starts with a cash sum and exchanges
it for income payments throughout your life. The modern,
but ugly, buzzword for this is 'decumulation'.

The only real disadvantage of an annuity is that if you die
fairly soon after buying the annuity, you will have paid a lot
of money for very few income payments in return (that is
why some people are willing to pay extra for a guaranteed
annuity). This is analogous to other types of insurance – you
could complain that house insurance premiums are always a
waste of money unless your house burns down! It's the
'swings and roundabouts' effect of insurance. What you are
buying with insurance is peace of mind that you are covered,
and what you are buying with an annuity is peace of mind
that you will still get your income no matter how long you
live. Bear in mind that you have roughly a 50% chance of
living longer than the average.

There are various options for how your annuity is structured.
Figure 7.1 assumed escalation of 3% and a 5-year guaranteed
period. You can vary either of these parameters, and this will
change the price of your annuity.

A level annuity stays the same every year. Escalation means
that your annuity increases each year by the amount
indicated – whether it is, for example, 3% or 5% or by the
retail price index (RPI). An escalating annuity always costs
more than a level one.

Another choice is to have your annuity guaranteed, whether
or not you die, for a fixed number of years. The most

common type of guarantee is for a fixed term, often five or ten years. The idea is that your estate is protected from the possibility that you apply a large cash sum (your pension pot) towards buying a pension, and then die early and receive very little benefit. If your pension is fixed for five years (or whatever term is available), the annuity will continue for at least that period whether or not you die.

As you can see from Figure 7.2, the level of escalation you choose makes a big difference to the initial amount of annuity you receive, but the effect of extending your guarantee period is relatively marginal.

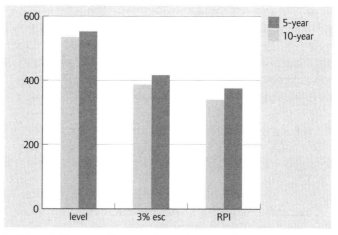

FIGURE 7.2: How annuities vary by options you choose
Monthly income for £100,000 invested. Male aged 65: level annuity, 3% escalation, RPI escalation. 5-year and 10-year guarantees.

Why take a guarantee?

The main reason that people will pay extra for a guarantee is that they (or their relatives) don't like the possibility of money being 'wasted' as a result of an early death. You have a free choice, but it will cost slightly more.

The most obvious situation in which you are likely to gain from a guarantee is where you strongly believe that you will only live a short time after retirement. If the pension options do not take account of your health (and you are not obliged to disclose anything), the guarantee could be quite valuable.

Joint annuities

So far we have talked in terms of your retirement, your annuity income and how the amount varies according to your lifespan. But if you have been the main breadwinner and your spouse will be spending your retirement with you, you probably want your annuity to reflect that situation too.

That's where 'joint' annuities come in: rather than the annuity just being paid for the duration of your life, it can be extended past the point of your death to provide a continuing income for your spouse.

Naturally, this will increase the price of your annuity (producing a lower overall annuity for the same pot). There are two things you can do to keep the increased cost as low as possible.

1 Structure the pension so that when one of you dies, the pension decreases to reflect lower total living costs. A reduction of one-third or a half is common (but watch out for fixed living costs that may not reduce when one of you dies, like house rental and the cost of running a car).

2 Your spouse will probably have their own state pension, and may also have pensions from other sources. This can be used to offset the total amount of annuity he or she would need if you die first.

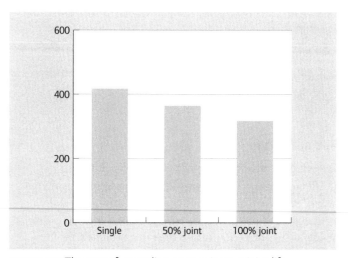

FIGURE 7.3: The cost of extending an annuity to a joint life
Monthly income for £100,000 invested. Male age 65, wife aged 62. Escalation 3%, guaranteed 5 years. Single life, 50% joint, 100% joint.

In Figure 7.3, the first column is the amount of annuity for a single man aged 65 with no joint annuity. The next two columns show that the initial annuity is lower if 50% of it continues after death for the benefit of the spouse, and lower still if 100% continues after the first death. In this example we have assumed a spouse age of 62 – the actual numbers quoted in each case will depend on the spouse's actual age.

Tricky language

We have used the single word 'joint' to describe extending your annuity for your spouse, but it is easy to be tripped up by the language because technically there are two types of joint annuity.

1 *The one we have just described is technically called 'joint life last survivor' (or 'joint life second death') because the annuity doesn't stop when the first person dies, it keeps going (possibly at a lower level) to pay the survivor an annuity. This the most common form of joint annuity.*

> 2 The other type is called 'joint life first death' and this refers to an annuity which stops as soon as either of the parties dies. This is cheaper because it terminates the annuity as early as possible, but is rarely as useful for the same reason.

State of health

A relatively recent development in annuity products has been to take your state of health into account, most commonly if you have been a smoker for most of your life. The morbid rationale is that because you have smoked you are much more likely to die sooner, so the insurance company can afford to pay you more each year. Some companies will also take other negative medical conditions into account, so if you are in poor health you can gain a modest amount of consolation by shopping around for improved annuity income.

The market for ill-health annuities is changing continuously and there are very few general rules – most companies in the market will quote on individual circumstances. However, the rates for the most common cause of ill health in annuity pricing – smoking – show that you could easily get an improvement of 20% to 25% in your annuity if you smoke.

If you are buying a purchased life annuity with your own cash (rather than through a pension) and are in poor health, you need to think about whether to buy an annuity at all. An annuity works best if you live a long time and so are able to receive lots of payments. If you are in seriously bad health and cannot find an insurer who fully recognises this in the annuity rate offered, you might do better to keep your cash.

Drawdown

Drawdown is an option halfway between managing your assets on a do-it-yourself basis and buying an annuity. Basically, you can decide to manage your assets for a limited period with the intention of buying an annuity later. Some of the reasons you might do this are the following:

▌ You have short-term income needs that are different from the long-term, so you don't want to set your income in stone by buying an annuity yet.

▌ Annuity rates are not attractive for you right now, and you think you will do better by waiting until they might improve.

Although there are drawdown (and related) products available as part of pensions planning, you don't need to buy one if you have non-pension assets – you just manage your funds as you wish and buy an annuity later on. In the next chapter we will describe drawdown products in more detail, but the main thing to remember is that drawdown carries more risk than buying an annuity now – your funds may not perform well and annuity rates could be worse in future than they are today.

Living off your assets

This is the 'luxury' option and is really only available to people who have a sufficiently large amount of assets that the investment returns by themselves are sufficient to cover any shortfall in retirement income.

It is potentially attractive because you don't eat into the capital itself: you just use the interest to add to your pension. This means that the original amount of capital is maintained, and can either be kept as a general purpose contingency fund for use later in life, or passed on as an inheritance.

This is how it works:

1 However much cash or capital you start with, you keep that amount. If you start with £500,000, say, you make sure that you always keep hold of the £500,000.

2 You don't keep it under the mattress. You invest it either in high-interest bank accounts or other secure investments. You would also be wise to spread it over a number of accounts to maximise the protection available under the FSCS (financial services compensation scheme) rules.

3 You only use the interest, dividends or other returns from your capital as income.

4 Several years later, your capital (e.g. the original £500,000) still remains. You can dip into it for emergencies or leave it as part of your estate to be inherited by the next generation when you pass away.

There are two keys to making this option work. First, you need to be able to satisfy yourself that you will generate sufficient investment returns to pay for the income that you need. And second, you need to be reasonably comfortable that whatever you invest in doesn't risk eroding your capital just when you need it (as the adverts keep telling us, stocks and shares can go down in value, as well as up).

Figure 7.4 shows some examples of the amount of income you might receive from investment returns alone compared to purchasing an annuity.

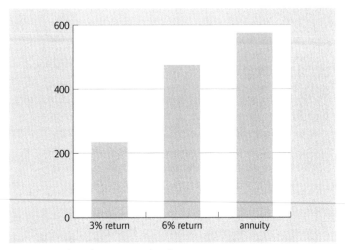

FIGURE 7.4: Annuity compared to investment returns
Monthly income for £100,000 invested. Male aged 65, level annuity, 5-year
guarantee. Compared to investment returns of 3% and 6%.

Figure 7.4 shows quite clearly how critical the investment
rate of return is to this option. However, if you can achieve a
reasonable income the advantage over an annuity is that you
keep your original capital.

There are three important things to bear in mind:

1. Once you have purchased an annuity, the income is
   guaranteed for your life – whereas investment returns can
   fluctuate over time.

2. If interest rates and investment returns rise in the market,
   that doesn't automatically mean that annuities are
   relatively worse value, because the amount you could get
   from an annuity would tend to rise too.

3. The amounts we have shown are before tax. All investment
   returns are normally taxed, while only a portion of a
   purchased life annuity is taxed. So after applying your own
   tax rate, the differences are likely to be greater than that
   illustrated in the figure.

Mix-and-match

None of the three methods for turning assets into income just described are mutually exclusive – you can mix and match them. For example, if you have total assets of £600,000 you could purchase an annuity with £200,000, use £200,000 for drawdown, leaving £200,000 for inheritance (while taking the interest and dividends). The numbers can get complicated very quickly, so it would be worthwhile to get professional advice if you are thinking about any of these options.

FSA advice about managing in retirement

▌ *Retirement can last 20–30 years, or even longer if you retire early, so you need to make your money go as far as possible.*

▌ *Boost your income by claiming your state benefits and checking what else is available.*

▌ *Trace any income you may have lost track of.*

▌ *Start an emergency fund if you don't have one.*

▌ *Check your tax allowances and tax code.*

Summary

▌ You can maximise your income by making sure that you claim all the benefits you are entitled to.

▌ You also need to recognise the possibility that you will need extra money in future to pay for some form of healthcare.

▌ You can use the value of your house to provide extra income – but this is complicated and could be expensive, so you need to be very careful.

▌ The easiest way to turn cash into a reliable income is to buy an annuity. Annuities are available in a wide variety of shapes and sizes, and new types are being designed all the time.

▌ There are various ways in which you can use other assets to provide an additional pension.

At the point of retirement

The big moment is approaching, so it may seem that there is little more you can do to secure the best possible retirement. In fact, there are quite a few key decisions you can take that would make a lot of difference.

The first decision is about how you make the transition. In the past we used to think of retirement as a one-off 'big bang' transition that moved us permanently from the world of work into the world of pipes and slippers. These days there is a lot more flexibility and you can take advantage of that flexibility to tailor your retirement arrangements to suit your own circumstances.

Having decided on the best retirement plan, you will have a number of decisions at each stage. We will guide you through some of the implications of these decisions so that you can arrange things to your maximum advantage.

What is retirement?

We used to think that retirement was an all-or-nothing affair, which involved leaving work one day at a retirement party, then staying at home and starting to receive a pension the very next day. Not any more. You have a lot more control over the timing of events regarding:

▌ when you stop working in your current job;

▌ whether you take another job when you have 'retired' from your current job;

▌ when and how you start to receive money from the main sources of pensions:

- the state,
- your current employer (and past employers),
- pensions and savings policies,
- other financial resources.

In practice, you have a high degree of control over all these factors so you can arrange them in many different combinations.

We used to think about work being one job or career for life with the same employer, but nowadays people think in terms of portfolio careers supported by transportable skills. Most of us still think of 'retirement' in its original sense: a single event at a single moment in time. So the idea that it's a messy combination of different decisions can feel uncomfortable at first – but is worth getting used to because it gives you a lot more choices.

So you can think of retirement as a timed sequence of different events, rather than a single big-bang event. Let's look at each of these different events in turn.

We will begin with the first half of the retirement equation – your options for when you choose to stop work. We will then look at the other half – when to start taking your pension.

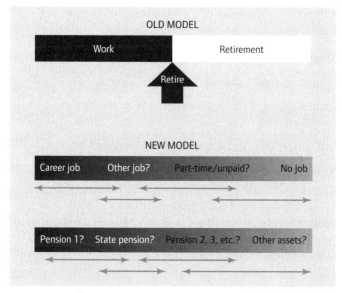

FIGURE 8.1: Different ways to think about retirement

When your employment stops

Introduction

When you originally signed your employment contract (and possibly joined your company pension scheme) you expected to retire at a specific age, normally 60 for women and 65 or 60 for men.

Employment law now requires employers to properly consider any request to work beyond the previously agreed retirement date; although the requirement is to consider the request, they are not forced to grant it. In practice, many employers are happy to grant a lot of flexibility around the date you stop work and the date you start to receive a company pension. Most employers will still think about stopping work and starting your pension as a single event, but even so it would be wise for you to keep these as separate events in your own mind for planning purposes.

Let's look at your possible choices in terms of when to stop working. There are three options:

1 Stop work at your expected retirement age;

2 Continue to work beyond your retirement age;

3 Retire earlier than your expected retirement age.

Stop work at your expected retirement age

Your expected retirement age is the one that is stipulated in your original employment contract and your company's pension scheme. Most employers automatically assume that you intend to retire at this age, and will have set up their administration arrangements on this basis – which may give you the impression that you have no choice.

You may positively wish to retire from your employment for a variety of reasons:

▌ there are things you are keen to do now that you can't do when you are still working;

▌ you have other work lined up;

▌ your employer is happy for you to retire but will still give you work on a less formal contract basis.

Work past your expected retirement age

You probably have more options than you thought. You do not have a statutory right to work past your retirement age, but you do have the right to request this and your employer must give proper consideration to your request. You may be able to negotiate a continuation of your employment on favourable terms for both parties, possibly to assist in the handover of your responsibilities to a successor. You should be prepared to be flexible about working part-time or reducing your salary, particularly if you are on a relatively high salary and you know that other work would pay less.

This has the obvious advantage that you can continue to earn money, which can go towards closing your pension gap. The main thing to be careful about is that your pension entitlement isn't damaged by taking a lower salary.

The ideal situation is when both you and your employer are keen for you to continue work. And if your employer is very keen, they may make it possible for you to continue to be in the pension scheme and so further increase your pension. This option is the 'dream ticket' from the point of view of closing your pension gap because it enables the pension turbocharger, which we explained earlier, to kick in. Just as a brief reminder, the pension turbocharger can boost your pension because of four different things:

1. More contributions are going into your pension pot if you stay within your company pension scheme.

2. Your pension pot is accumulating more investment returns.

3. Each £1 in your pension pot will buy you a higher pension (because you are retiring later, the pot is spread over a shorter expected number of years' retirement).

4. You are continuing to earn money, some of which can be used to boost your pension further or eliminate future drains on your pension (for example, paying off personal loans).

Even if your employer makes it difficult for you to stay on in your current job, you can get many of the advantages of retiring later by finding another job elsewhere and continuing to work. You may be able to 'defer' your pension until you are ready, or simply put the pensions money aside for later. These options are explored more fully when we talk about when to take your pension, later in this chapter.

Retire earlier than your expected retirement age

You don't have a statutory right to retire early – and in most circumstances this would be a bad idea anyway – but there may be exceptions. It's normally a bad idea because the pension turbocharger starts to operate in reverse and this can seriously reduce your pension pot. The main reasons for this are the following:

1. Both you and your employer will have paid less into your pension pot.

2. Your pension pot will have less time to get the benefit of investment returns.

3. Each £1 in your pension pot buys less pension: because you will be retired for a longer period than expected, your pension pot has to stretch further.

4. Your income will drop from the level of your salary to the level of your pension, so you will have less cash to close your pension gap in other ways.

Ill-health retirement

If you are in ill health, your pension scheme may permit you to retire early without penalty. Pension schemes can sometimes take a fairly liberal view of the definition of ill health, particularly if they have the backing of the company. (Conversely, some schemes have very tight definitions of ill health in their rules.) Just one word of caution: if you retire on ill-health grounds and decide to take another job, you would need to make sure that your ill-health pension isn't undermined by doing so.

Redundancy

If your employer is going through a downsizing programme, you may be offered advantageous terms to retire early, either through a redundancy payment or an improvement to your pension. The immediate cash from a redundancy payment can sometimes look attractive, but it's quite possible that any improved pension terms on offer will be worth more to you. People tend to underestimate the real value of a pension, so it is worth pausing and checking. It is difficult to make a precise pound-for-pound comparison because it depends on the precise terms of the pension being offered. The best bet is probably to ask your HR department whether they can obtain a rough valuation of the pension offered, and then decide.

Employers often prefer to incentivise redundancies through the pension scheme because the 'hit' on their accounts is less painful than immediate cash – which is why they might be inclined to be more generous. If an improvement to your pension is not initially offered it may be worth raising it as part of your redundancy negotiations, even if that means trading some of your redundancy cash.

Employer goodwill

In exceptional cases, it may even be possible that your employer is so grateful to you for the service you have given that they will 'uplift' your pension entitlement as a form of thank-you. If this is offered to you, make sure that you are suitably appreciative!

Resigning

Probably the worst action you can take if you wish to retire early is to resign. Your earnings will stop immediately and you are taking pot luck on whether your pension arrangements are flexible enough to allow the pension to be taken early (we will discuss your options on this shortly).

If your employer is not prepared to ease the way, the pension turbocharger will act against you and probably generate a large financial penalty. So even if you don't enjoy your current job, if you are in a company pension scheme and reasonably close to retirement, the best thing is probably to hang on.

Early retirement – summary

In a situation where you can retire early without damaging your pension it may well be worth doing so, particularly if you can get another job. You will be receiving your full pension as well as your work earnings for the period until you stop work, and may be able to put extra money aside to reduce your pensions gap.

Both the pension and earnings would be taxable, but new contributions to an extra pension for the future would attract tax relief in the normal way.

When your pension starts

We have just described how you probably have a lot of flexibility about when you stop work. Using this flexibility can help to reduce your pensions gap.

Similarly, you have more flexibility than you probably thought about when you start to receive your pension. In general terms the longer you can hold off taking your pension the higher it is likely to be, but of course there are all sorts of 'ifs' and 'buts' that you will need to think about.

Types of pension

The impact of changing the trigger point for starting your pensions payments depends on the source of your pension. We will look at each of the major sources in turn:

▋ State pensions

▋ Company pensions

▋ Personal pensions.

State pensions

For many years, the state pension age remained at 65 for men and 60 for women. But this has recently started to change, partly because of sexual equality laws and partly because of the ever-increasing cost of paying for state pensions.

The government will write to you four months before you reach state pension age with information about the options open to you. You will need to take this into account when looking at how much you will be receiving from other sources. For the moment, we will focus on the limited options you have about taking your state pension.

The main option on offer is that if you defer your basic state pension for a number of years, the amount of pension will increase. (The terms of this are likely to vary over time – current information is available from our website, **www.thepensionscrisis.com**.) In simple terms, the government is itself recognising the impact of the pension turbocharger and allowing it to operate in a limited form so that people can work longer than their normal retirement date if they wish to.

There is another simple option you can take if you want to continue to work but don't like the look of this 'deferment' option. You can receive your pension, and pay it into a separate bank account, or even use it to buy a personal pension which you can take later. This has the great merit of flexibility: you can choose exactly when to start using the money rather than working to the government's fairly arbitrary alternative.

When state pension is paid

At the moment, you can claim your state pension from the age of 60 if you are a woman born on or before 5 April 1950, and from 65 if you are a man.

Women's state pension age will rise to 65 between 2010 and 2020. For women born between 6 April 1950 and 5 April 1955, the state pension age will depend on the date of birth. From 6 April 2020, the state pension age for a woman will be the same as for a man.

From 2024, the state pension age for both men and women will gradually increase from 65 to reach 68 in 2046.

A new choice has also been introduced: if you decide to defer your pension the amount you receive, at your later retirement, will be increased.

Depending on how long you put off claiming your state pension for, you can choose to receive either:

▌ *extra state pension each week when you claim your state pension for the rest of your life, or*

▌ *a one-off, lump-sum payment plus your normal weekly state pension.*

As an example, in 2009, if you were entitled to a state pension of £100 per week, this would increase to £150 per week if you delayed retiring by five years. Up-to-date information about how much you can claim if you defer your state pension can be obtained from The Pensions Service or via **www.thepensioncrisis.com**.

Company pensions

By definition, if you are in a company pension scheme, your membership is linked to your contract of employment. Both your employment contract and the pension scheme will have the same 'normal retirement date' (NRD) stipulated in them. This is based on the reasonable assumption that once you cease employment on your NRD, you will wish to start receiving your pension at the same NRD.

But legally, your employment contract and your pension schemes are different entities. This is a deliberate part of pension scheme legislation, which was designed to protect the interests of the pension scheme members even if the company failed. Although your employer sets up the pension scheme, legally they have no control of the money once it is inside the scheme.

A pension scheme is governed by its own trustees, who are a mix of company-appointed and independent people whose task is to look after the interest of the members of the pension scheme. They are generally either members or pensioners of the scheme themselves. In recent years the power and responsibilities of trustees have increased. This has happened in response to the past actions of some employers who, illegally, attempted to use pension scheme money as if it were their own.

Despite all this, the company still has some influence on how its pension scheme operates, because it is making a large financial contribution which the scheme is dependent on.

So even if you are in a company pension scheme the distinction between 'stopping work' and 'starting to receive a pension', mentioned earlier in this chapter, is still valid. Strictly speaking, any negotiations about when you stop work have to be held with your employer, while any negotiations about when and how you receive your pension have to be held with the trustees of your pension scheme. In practice, your Human Resources department probably has a streamlined process for managing both at once.

The pension scheme will have a set of rules that determine how it acts in most situations, so these rules will be the first port of call if you want to change how you receive the pension you are entitled to.

Personal pensions

By contrast, a personal pension scheme is a direct contract between you and your pension company. You own the contract. As a result you have a lot more control over when you make and stop contributions, and when you retire. The main restriction is that until 6 April 2010 you cannot take your pension before age 50. After that you will not be able to take a pension before you are 55. (There are a couple of exceptions: you will still be able to retire early due to poor health, and if you have the right to retire before 50 at 6 April 2006, that right may be protected.)

The main thing is that you are relatively free to choose when you start your pension, irrespective of when you retire from your job.

Money purchase schemes

A company money purchase pension scheme is linked to your employment and normally has scheme rules which define when you can retire, and this will be linked to the retirement date in your employment contract. Normally you're expected to retire at this age and take your pension.

On the other hand, this type of scheme has similarities to a personal pension because you can point to an amount in your personal pot and say 'This is mine'. Like a personal pension, the amount you get will be determined by the amount that gets put in and the investment returns (less costs) that get applied. This means that it is much easier for a money purchase scheme to be flexible about when you take your pension.

As we have explained previously, you could seek to keep working past your normal retirement date. And if you have a pension gap, you will want to keep your pension pot in action and keep contributing to it for as long as possible. You may be able to continue to pay into your company money purchase pension long after the stipulated retirement date, especially if the scheme is a 'group personal pension' (which is, as we said earlier, a collection of separate personal pensions).

The one thing that you cannot guarantee is that your employer will continue to make contributions on your behalf after the stipulated retirement date. You can try and negotiate this – particularly if you remain in employment – but it would be a negotiation rather than a contractual entitlement.

Options for taking your pension

Tax-free cash

You (and your employer) are entitled to tax relief on contributions to your pension, but eventually when you receive the pension it is taxable as normal income.

However, there is a historical anomaly in the tax system that permits you to take part of your pension pot in cash without paying any tax on it at all. It is perfectly legal and proper to do so, and the advantage is that you save the tax that you would have paid had it stayed as a pension. The documentation you receive when you are about to trigger your pension should make this option clear and easy to exercise. You can currently take up to 25% of your pension pot as tax-free cash.

For obvious reasons this benefit has been known for many years as 'tax-free cash', and, since this is still the most commonly used name, it is the one we will continue to use. However, the government now refers to it as 'Pension Commencement Lump Sum' for reasons best known to itself.

The advantage of taking tax-free cash are self-evident, a nice lump sum to kick-start your retirement plans or pay down any debts. However, there are some drawbacks which we will consider shortly.

Money purchase pensions (including personal pensions) work by building up a cash pot. So when you take tax-free cash, the amount is simply deducted from the pot and the remainder is used to buy your pension.

Final salary schemes, on the other hand, normally offer you an amount of pension based on your final salary. If you want to take tax-free cash, some of this pension has to be sacrificed and converted into a cash amount.

Some final salary pension schemes, particularly in the public sector, build up a pension but also accumulate a completely separate tax-free cash 'pot'. The calculation is usually based on years of service and final salary, but with a different 'accrual rate' to allow for the fact that this is cash rather than a pension.

For either type of final salary scheme, you may be offered the chance to convert some of your pension into tax-free cash, up to the maximum level permitted. This looks like an automatic thing to do, but you need to pause and look carefully at the possible drawbacks we discuss in the next section.

Possible drawbacks of tax-free cash

First, if you already have a significant pension gap then taking the cash will reduce your pension – and increase the gap. The temptation to spend the cash on a party or a new car will be huge. The trick here is to simply reinvest the cash in another investment (but not another pension) that will pay you an income to make up for the drop in pension. In theory, you will still be better off by the amount of tax you have saved.

But that leads us to the second possible drawback. If you have a money purchase pension plan or scheme, your pension pot will already be expressed in terms of cash accumulated, so taking cash out is a simple and clean transaction. But if you are in a final salary pension scheme your entitlement is defined in terms of an amount of pension, so if you want to take cash the scheme will have to convert from pension into cash. (This also applies if your scheme accrues separate tax-free cash and you are offered more by sacrificing some pension.) There are no set rules that pension schemes have to use for this conversion, so it is quite possible for them to be less than generous.

We introduced the concept of your 'pension price' in Chapter 4, and also explained that it could work in reverse – this is an example of that. Suppose that you worked out that your pension price is 25 – in other words you would have to pay £25,000 for every £1,000 of pension. If your pension scheme offers you £10,000 of tax-free cash for every £1,000 of pension that you give up that is clearly a poor deal for you, no matter how much tax relief you can get on the cash. (This example may look extreme but in reality it isn't – trustees of final salary schemes have a lot of extraneous factors to take into account when they make this sort of offer.)

Complaints and advice

This calculation is a bit tricky, so probably the simplest thing to do is show the example to your pensions administrator and ask them whether you may be losing some of the gains from the tax relief by converting. You should get an honest answer, even if it is one that you don't like.

If that doesn't work, you will have to ask a financial adviser to work out the numbers for you, and expect to pay for their advice. (Information on choosing an adviser is contained in Chapter 12.)

All pension schemes have dispute resolution procedures, and you can get external advice from the Pensions Advisory Service – see our website for a link.

Purchasing your pension

If you have any form of money purchase pension, when you retire you have accumulated a fixed amount of cash in your pension and need to use it to buy your pension either from your insurance company, or by taking the 'open market option' (see below). Bear in mind that any tax-free cash that you take will reduce the amount of money available to buy your pension.

Much like with a purchased life annuity, you can buy a pension annuity with escalation, guarantees, and joint life options – these were described more fully in the previous chapter.

Open market option

We just discussed taking tax-free cash, and how the conversion from pension to cash could catch you out. Converting from cash to pension could catch you out too! Here is how you can avoid this happening.

We mentioned that if you have a money purchase pension (whether it is a personal pension or company pension scheme), the pension pot is defined in terms of a cash amount. When you retire, this cash is then converted into your pension: it effectively 'buys' the pension. A common problem is that the company or scheme your pension is with will not necessarily have the most generous conversion terms on the market. It's exactly the same problem that we described for tax-free cash, but in reverse.

But this time, there is a solution. By law, all pension companies and schemes are obliged to offer you an 'open market option' (OMO) which enables you to shop around and get the best possible pension terms on the market. Consumer groups and the FSA have campaigned about the low take-up rate of open market options, much of which is caused by apathy and lack of awareness. Just to repeat, this is a legal right that you are entitled to and is a potentially valuable way

of increasing your pension. The difference it makes to your pension varies, but at the time of writing OMOs could be more than 30% better than the pension offered by your pension provider
(see Figure 8.2).

In the past, some companies tried to charge a penalty for exercising the option, a practice which the financial regulators now frown upon. If your pension documentation isn't clear about your rights or you find obstacles being put in

Don't lose your OMO!

If you have any form of money purchase pension, exercising your open market option could be one of the most effective ways of increasing your pension. If you don't exercise it, you could lose money for no good reason – yet in 2008 the FSA reported that 60% of eligible people didn't use their OMO. They could easily have lost a lot of money because of this. Don't be one of them!

your way, press on and if necessary complain.

Your open market option is obviously of most value if you can get a higher pension by shopping around. This is highly likely if, sadly, you are in sufficiently poor health that you are likely to have fewer years to live than the average person.

Most pension schemes and insurance companies assume everyone is in average health and do their calculations on this basis. They are simply not geared up to vary their terms by individual state of health – but a competitive open marketplace is.

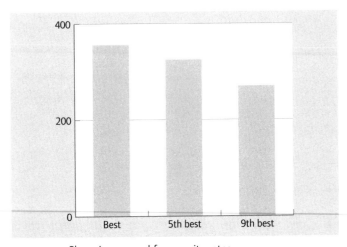

FIGURE 8.2: Shopping around for annuity rates

Monthly income for £100,000 invested. Comparison of best, 5th best and 9th best annuity rate. Male aged 65, 3% escalation, 5-year guarantee, joint life 50%.

The differences in rates for people who are in good health can be quite dramatic. Figure 8.2 was based on nine of the most active annuity companies who provide live rate updates to the FSA and other websites. The best annuity is over 30% higher than the worst within just this limited group of companies. You might be lucky enough to be with one of those companies with the best rates, but it is worth checking. And remember that these numbers do not allow for your state of health – if this is poor, the gap between your current provider and the best available rate could be even wider.

Conversely, there is little point using your option to shop around if the sums involved are small. If you have a pot of less than, say, £20,000, you might find that any gain in rates is outweighed by the cost and effort of transferring your pension. It's also quite possible that your pension provider already offers a competitive rate.

If you have a reasonable amount in your pension pot, the wisest thing is to get an OMO quote and just check whether you can get a better pension by buying it elsewhere.

State pensions and final salary schemes

You have very few immediate options with final salary schemes and the state pension, because the benefits are already defined in terms of an amount of pension (rather than a cash pension pot that you have to convert into a pension).

The state pension automatically increases each year in line with price inflation.

Most 'final salary' schemes already have an element of inflation-proofing built into them. This is either because that is the way they have been designed (most public sector pension schemes are inflation-proofed), or because the trustees regularly review the level of pensions against inflation, and make adjustments.

In the past, when final salary schemes have had surpluses, trustees have sometimes even improved the overall level of pensions above inflation – although this has not happened much recently because the pensions crisis and recent investment performance has left most schemes in deficit.

Drawdown

There are circumstances in which, rather than converting cash into income now, it could be advantageous to 'do it yourself' for a limited period: this is commonly referred to as 'income withdrawal' or 'drawdown'. Examples of situations where drawdown might be useful are the following:

▎ your income needs for the first few years are significantly different from what you expect later;

▎ by reducing your income in some years, you may be able to reduce your liability to income tax;

▎ if annuity rates are very poor when your retire, and you expect them to improve later;

▌ you believe you are in poor health but cannot prove it to an insurance company yet; by delaying an annuity purchase you might receive a higher income.

This is how drawdown works:

1 You don't buy an annuity straight away. You keep all your cash as cash (or short-term investments) for now.

2 You spend as much (or as little) as you need for a number of years. This is the 'drawdown' period. Naturally this is a drain on your cash, so you spend as little as you can get away with!

3 When things are more stable, you use the remaining cash to buy an annuity – to provide an income for the remainder of your life.

By adopting this hybrid approach you are gaining more flexibility by carrying some of the short-term risk yourself. However, you still avoid the worst risk of all: living a long life but running out of the cash that you need to enjoy it.

The important thing is to have a plan, limit the drawdown period and take the minimum possible income so that there is sufficient cash left at the end of the period to buy the annuity that you will need for the remainder of your life. If you spend too much during the drawdown period you will leave an insufficient cash sum at the end and will be worse off than if you had bought an annuity right at the start.

Some pension policies offer a very similar facility built into the pension plan itself. Instead of buying a fixed pension at retirement you can 'drawdown' from your pension pot for a few years (subject to limits), and buy a pension later. Fixed pensions have to be bought by age 75 because of pensions rules.

Planning whether to use drawdown is one of the more complex and far-reaching options around your pension choices, and it is essential that you get professional advice when making your decisions.

> ### FSA guidelines for drawdown (and similar products)
>
> *Even though drawdown or phased retirement have some advantages, they also carry risks and are complex so you should obtain advice before taking action.*
>
> *Additional charges for the facility could be high, and these could wipe out any gains unless the fund is sufficiently large (probably at least £100,000).*
>
> *You need to be aware that you are taking two risks with your pension:*
>
> 1. *you are keeping some of your pension in a fund, and this could perform poorly;*
> 2. *you are making a bet on future annuity rates – they could be better than today, but they could also be worse.*

Phased retirement and flexible annuities

Phased retirement (sometimes known as staggered vesting) is a halfway house between drawdown and taking your pension straight away. Your pension fund is divided into 1,000 segments and each year you decide which segments are converted into pension income and which remain to grow further within the pension fund.

Flexible annuity products are similar to drawdown in that they allow you to defer the purchase of the fixed annuity. They are technically issued as annuities, but the returns are not guaranteed – your funds are invested in a range of equity and fixed interest funds and you take an income in the short term. Later on, the remaining funds are used to purchase an annuity at rates ruling at that time.

New annuity and annuity-like products are being developed all the time, and it is beyond the scope of this book to describe them all.

Immediate vesting

'Immediate vesting' is a technical term for a straightforward, and legal, device that can enhance your financial situation in the year that you retire. It works like this:

1. You make a lump sum contribution into a pension plan from any other cash that you have available (for example, savings that are not already invested in a pension plan).

2. As long as the contribution is within the normal tax limits, it attracts basic rate tax relief.

3. If you are a higher rate taxpayer, you can include the contribution in your tax returns and obtain further tax relief.

4. You trigger (or 'vest') your retirement under your pension plan immediately.

5. You take the maximum tax-free cash lump sum from the pension plan (currently 25%), plus the normal yearly pension payments.

If you don't already have a pension plan that will permit you to invest the extra cash immediately before retirement, you can purchase a special 'immediate vesting' personal pension plan that has been designed for this purpose.

Because you are receiving tax relief on this extra contribution but immediately received some of it back in terms of tax-free cash, you are effectively receiving an extra bonus from the taxman that you would not have got otherwise.

Here is an example of immediate vesting. A man aged 65 has £40,000 in (non-pension) savings. As long as he is within the limits (see Chapter 5) he can invest this in a pension and tax relief will gross up his contribution to £50,000.

He vests the pension immediately and takes 25% tax-free cash of £12,500. This leaves £37,500 in the pension, which is used to buy an annuity of £2,616 per annum.

The net result is that he has paid out £27,500 in cash (£40,000 less the tax-free cash of £12,500) for an annual income of £2,616. This represents a guaranteed yield of 9.5% per annum, much higher than the basic annuity yield of 5.2% that underpins the calculation. If he is a higher-rate taxpayer, he may also be able to obtain higher-rate tax relief which would increase the yield further – to 14.9% on the same basis.

There are a couple of caveats. You start with cash, and you will end up with a smaller amount of cash plus an annual pension – so you need to make sure that you are happy to exchange some of your cash now for an income in the future. You also have to be careful to make sure that the costs of the transaction and the likely returns from the pension don't take a huge chunk out of the tax bonus.

Although immediate vesting is perfectly legitimate, it clearly requires specialist knowledge to make sure that it is being done correctly. We strongly recommend that you take advice either from your accountant or financial adviser.

FSA advice

▌ *You don't have to stop working to convert your personal fund into a pension.*

▌ *You cannot convert before you are 50 (going up to 55 by 2010) and you must convert them on your 75th birthday at the latest.*

▌ *Find out whether you'll be penalised if you don't buy an annuity at your stated retirement age.*

▶

- *Check whether you could get a better income because of your health, lifestyle, occupation or where you live.*

- *Think very carefully about the type of annuity you want, as you can't change your mind once you've bought it.*

- *You can take up to a quarter of your pension fund in cash, as a tax-free lump sum before your 75th birthday.*

- *If you're in an occupational pension scheme, it may have different rules about when a pension can be taken – check with your scheme administrators.*

- *If the total of all your pension funds is less than a minimum amount, you can take a cash lump sum instead of an income. You must be at least 60 but not yet reached 75 and you have to convert all your pension funds to cash within a 12-month period.*

Summary

- We used to think of retirement as a fixed single event, but that no longer needs to be the case.

- By thinking of leaving work and starting your pension as two separate and movable events, you generate much more flexibility in how you can reduce your pension gap.

- You can structure your pension in many different ways, and it is worth giving some serious thought to how you can tailor your pension to your own circumstances.

- You don't have to buy your annuity from your pension provider. Exercising an OMO (open market option) might get you a significantly larger pension.

Close to retirement (50s and 60s)

If you are in your 50s or 60s but have not yet retired, you should be taking a lot of interest in the pensions crisis. You have probably started thinking about planning for retirement and there is a good chance that you have a pension gap – but you still have time to do something about it. If you let things drift now you may be losing valuable opportunities to improve your situation.

The starting point is to get a rough idea of how big your pension gap is (see Chapter 6). If you have been in some form of final salary pension scheme and have stayed with the same employer for most of your career, your pension gap is likely to be small.

If, on the other hand, you are like most of the population and have changed employment a fair bit and spent time working in jobs which don't have generous final salary schemes, you could well have a substantial gap.

The pension turbocharger

In Chapter 4 ('Inside Information') we described how the pension turbocharger works. Briefly, when you retire later, the pension you eventually get could increase much faster than you might think – because of the turbocharger effect. But you also have to be careful because the turbocharger works in reverse too: if you retire earlier your pension could be severely damaged.

We looked at the impact of the pension turbocharger on decisions at the point of retirement in the last chapter. But if you have more time before you retire, you have a lot more time to think through the potential impact of the turbocharger and make decisions sufficiently in advance to get the maximum benefit from it.

In simple terms, if you have a pension gap, one of the most effective things you can do is to turbocharge your pension by retiring later. Keep this in mind as you consider the options in this chapter.

Pensions are generated from a number of different sources:

1. state pensions;
2. company pensions;
3. personal pensions;
4. tax-free savings products like ISAs (and its predecessors TESSAs and PEPs);
5. your own income and assets.

So let's do what we can to increase the amount of pension you might receive from each of these sources.

State pensions

When it comes to the state pension your options are fairly limited, but let's look at what they are.

You can defer your retirement date for up to five years and receive either extra pension or an extra cash sum.

The terms are not particularly advantageous, but they are reasonably fair. If you are planning on retiring later anyway it might be worth you deferring your state pension so that all your pensions start at the same time, but financially the decision is fairly neutral.

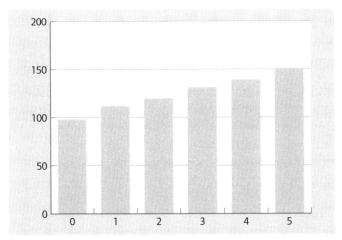

FIGURE 9.1: Effect of deferring your state pension
How a state pension of £100 rises if it is deferred. 1, 2, 3, 4 and 5 years.

There are a couple of things to watch out for here. First, for every year that you defer your pension, you give up some pension now but hope to gain it later through the higher amount of pension that is paid in the future. If you are in poor health, that could be a poor bargain – so you might as well enjoy the pension now.

Second, the idea looks sensible and simple but, as is so common with government initiatives, its implementation is surrounded by a huge number of ifs and buts. The Pensions Service leaflet on deferral of state pensions runs to over 100 pages. If you have the energy, a link is available on our website.

The only other way that you can effectively boost your state pension is to qualify for means-tested benefits (known as Pension Credit). Hopefully, even if you have a pension gap, your financial situation is not close to this situation – but if it is you do need to be careful. In effect, if you qualify for Pension Credit, a large part of every £1 of assets that you are able to secure by yourself is taken away by the government – for more information see Chapter 5.

Company pensions

When thinking about company pensions, the first thing to do is to cast your mind back and think about the companies you have worked for in the past. Even if you can't remember whether you were a member of a pension scheme and don't have any papers to hand, it's worth contacting them because the trustees of every scheme are very diligent about keeping their own records. This is still so if a company has been taken over by another: any pension that you are entitled to is unlikely to have been affected. There is nothing to lose and everything to gain from checking with your old employers.

Once you have been able to locate your old company, just send them a letter to check whether you are entitled to any pension. A sample letter is available at our website, **www.thepensionscrisis.com**.

Turning to your current employer, the most important thing is to check whether they have a pension scheme and, if so, that you are participating in it to the maximum possible extent. This means making the maximum possible contributions that you are entitled to make, but also exploring whether you are able to make additional voluntary contributions (AVCs). You could make extra pension provision over and above your pension scheme by buying a personal pension, but the charges in AVC schemes are normally lower.

One of the options that some final salary pension schemes offer is to take cash (known as a 'transfer value') in from your old company schemes and in exchange enhance your benefits in your current company scheme. This transfer value is the amount that the old scheme is prepared to pay to remove you from its future liabilities. In effect, the transfer value is the current market value of the pension benefits that you have built up in the old scheme. Normally, pension schemes are keen to be more generous to people who stay in the scheme than people who leave early. So you shouldn't necessarily expect the transfer value from your old scheme to buy much in terms of new pension benefits in your new scheme. (A transfer value must be paid directly into another pension plan: it can never be paid directly to you.)

If it agrees, your current scheme will normally offer you a number of extra years' service for pension purposes. This means that if you expected to work through your current employer for, say, 10 years, then they might grant an extra 3 or 4 years' 'pensionable service' in exchange for receiving the cash transfer value. If you are in a generous pension scheme which enhances benefits regularly, or if you expect your salary to increase fairly rapidly in this job, this can be very advantageous. It's ultimately a judgment call, but you can make an intelligent judgment by looking at projections of what you may get (both your old and new schemes will provide projections) and assess which ones are likely to turn out better.

FSA advice on transfers

▌ *If you decide to transfer, your employer must first convert the benefits you have built up in the pension scheme into a monetary value, called a cash-equivalent transfer value.*

▌ *You must then invest the transfer value in another scheme or plan or use it to purchase a buy-out contract.*

▌ *A buy-out contract (also sometimes called a section 32 contract) is an individual insurance policy that will provide pension benefits to you in the future. The benefits you receive may depend on the performance of the investments in the policy.*

▌ *Not all employer pension schemes accept transfers, so check first.*

Salary sacrifice

If you are employed, your employer may have a 'salary sacrifice' scheme – which is one way of increasing the funding to your pension with minimum cost to you and your employer. The basic mechanism is that you voluntarily take a lower salary, thereby reducing both your own and your employer's national insurance contributions. Your employer can then use this saving and your salary reduction to purchase your pension.

As an example, if you were on a salary of £25,000 per annum and could afford to pay £100 gross a month into your pension, you could instead opt for salary sacrifice if it were offered – reducing your salary to about £23,600. Your net income would stay exactly the same. If your employer passes on the full savings on tax and your own national insurance contributions, the pension contribution could rise to over £115 per month. If your employer also passes on its own savings from national insurance (not all do) this could rise to over £130 per month.

The advantage is clear from the example: an increase of up to 30% in pension contributions at no cost to you in the short term. The savings are likely to be lower for higher earning employees because of the additional 1% NI paid on earnings in excess of £40,040 (2008–09). While on the surface this looks like an obvious thing to do for both you and your employer, you need to realise that this is a material change to your employment contract – and a lower salary might impact on other benefits that are based on salary: e.g. bonus payments, salary increases, overtime, etc. You should talk to your HR department to understand the full implications of this option in your own circumstances.

Changing jobs

When you are thinking about changing jobs and moving from one company pension scheme into another, you are in a stronger negotiating position than if you are a continuing employee. There are several ways that you can exercise this negotiating power without necessarily antagonising your new employer. This is because any concessions made by your new employer show up in the company pension scheme rather than immediately in the company accounts.

Clearly, if you are going through a routine recruitment process for a relatively junior role, you will have very limited scope for the sort of possibilities we describe below, but it's worthwhile being aware of them just in case.

If you are extremely fortunate and in a situation where your new employer is very keen to hire you and is looking for ways to enhance your total package, one of the most elegant things to negotiate is an enhancement to the level of pension benefits that your transfer value (discussed above) will purchase. For example, if you were in your previous scheme for six years your transfer value may only buy you two years in your new scheme. You might be able to negotiate more than two years in your new scheme, repairing some of the damage that leaving your old scheme early may have caused to your pension.

Even if you don't have a transfer value from previous schemes, you may still be able to negotiate better pension benefits in the form of 'enhanced accrual'. This means that each single future year of service is agreed to count for two or three years (or whatever number you can negotiate) in terms of future pension accrual. The justification for this is that when someone is enticed to leave an old pension scheme they lose pension benefits, so it is fair for the new company to make them up.

Finally, you may be able to take advantage of the way that 'salary sacrifice', which we just described above, works. In this case you are not physically reducing your salary (because you don't have one yet), just negotiating a lower prospective salary in exchange for higher pension benefits. The benefits of reduced national insurance works in the same way, and the same caveats about the impact of a lower salary apply.

If your new employer is able to win the support of the scheme trustees (which should not be taken for granted) to these enhancements, it can be attractive because it is actually paid for by the pension scheme – which is funded by the employer over a long period. So it avoids the immediate costs, and possible pay pressure from other employees, that a higher salary would entail. Once again, this type of thing is only likely in exceptional circumstances, so don't raise your hopes too high!

Personal pensions

As with company pensions, the first thing to do with personal pensions is to find out how many you have. Try and remember whether you have ever taken out a personal pension policy in the past and, if possible, get hold of the paperwork. Even if you stopped paying premiums many years ago, there is a good chance that the policy still has a residual value; in most cases personal pension policies are never actually cancelled if premiums cease: they are converted into what is known as 'paid up'. There has been a lot of consolidation of life assurance companies (who are the main providers of personal pensions) over the last couple of decades, so one of your tasks might be to track down who currently holds your old pension policies. The DWP pension tracing service may be a useful first step (**www.thepensionservice.gov.uk**). Once you have tracked them down, you can write using one of our draft letters, available on our website.

Prior to 2000 many companies were accused of mis-selling personal pensions and have had to pay compensation. Most claims for mis-selling are now 'timed out' because companies have already been through an extensive programme of contacting customers and compensating them if appropriate. But if you have reason to believe that you were mis-sold and didn't have the chance to claim for some reason, contact the company concerned and they will tell you what options you have.

Tax-free savings products

The first thing to do is to start thinking about all of your income and assets as being available to fund your retirement.

Next, you need to decide what to do with them so that they are working as hard as possible for you. The most obvious thing to do is to make sure that as many of your assets as possible are sheltered (legally) from taxation.

As described previously, a pension plan is the most obvious way to gain tax relief and put assets away for retirement. Despite the obvious advantages, pension plans do have a significant disadvantage. They limit your flexibility: once your cash is inside a pension plan you cannot get hold of it until you have retired (when you can get the cash back in the form of an initial tax-free cash payment plus future pension payments). More flexible pension products have been developed in recent years (like 'drawdown' pensions, which are discussed elsewhere in this book), but it's still not possible to withdraw cash at a moment's notice to deal with an emergency.

ISAs are general-purpose savings plans that also attract tax relief, and at the time of writing you can invest up to £7,200 a year in an ISA. You have a range of choices about where the money can be invested, but the key point is that you are not required to purchase a pension (although you could do so if you wish) and can access the cash at any time. You may also have built up funds in the predecessors to ISAs – PEPs and TESSAs. You can take income from these funds free of tax, so they are worth ring-fencing from spending until you are in retirement.

Neither pensions nor ISAs are the clear best choice: if you have sufficient assets, then a judicious mix of the two will provide a high level of tax relief (through the pension) while retaining a degree of flexibility for unforeseen circumstances (through the ISA).

Pension or ISA?

ISAs are an attractive alternative to using a pension plan to save for your retirement because they combine flexibility with the availability of tax relief. Key points to bear in mind are:

▍ *You can set up one ISA for each tax year up to the contribution limit for that year. Ideally, you need to remember to set up an ISA every year (or sign up to an ISA that automatically renews every year).*

▍ *The yearly contribution limits on ISAs are much lower than on pensions (although over time it may be possible to build up a large ISA fund).*

▍ *Unlike pensions, you don't get tax relief on an ISA contribution – just on the interest and investment returns on your savings. Conversely you don't pay tax on the proceeds once you take them.*

▍ *If you are a higher-rate taxpayer now, and expect to be a basic rate taxpayer in retirement, a pension has a tax advantage over an ISA because you get higher rate relief on your contributions (up to the current limits) but will only pay basic rate tax on your pension.*

▍ *ISAs count as part of your total assets should you lose your job and apply for benefits or go bankrupt. Pensions are protected in both these situations.*

'Lifestyling'

Until now, you will probably have had a degree of exposure to the stock market in your pension pot. This is entirely appropriate to maximise your investment returns and grow your capital. However, as you move towards retirement, now is the time to consider switching into less risky funds such as bonds and cash to reduce your exposure to the market and lock in any gains you have made. You don't want to take the chance of the market dropping significantly in the run-up to your planned retirement date. Conversely, if you will not need to realise cash to purchase an annuity (because you intend to use drawdown or a related product), this may not be an issue. You need to discuss this with your accountant or financial adviser.

Some pension products already have this feature built in – the jargon name is 'lifestyling'. At its simplest this could mean the ability to switch your assets from the stock market to less volatile deposit-type funds before you are forced to cash in at retirement. There are also more complex facilities that allow a gradual transition over a period of time.

You may be fortunate enough to have other income or assets which can be used to partially fund your retirement. You may for example have a 'buy-to-let' property. The key thing is to maintain your flexibility so that you are not forced to liquidate any assets when their value is depressed due to market conditions.

Liabilities

We naturally tend to think of assets and investments when we think about providing for retirement, but it's also worth thinking about your liabilities and how you plan to eliminate these before you retire.

Your mortgage is likely to be your biggest liability so it is worth thinking about how you can eliminate it. If you have an 'interest only' mortgage you will only have been repaying the interest so you need to consider what you have in place to repay the capital. If you have taken out an endowment policy for this purpose, you may find it is now projected to pay out less than the outstanding mortgage. In this case, you need to think about what other assets you can use to make up the shortfall.

Many mortgages these days have some flexibility to allow you to make additional penalty-free payments (either regular or one-offs) to accelerate the repayment of the mortgage. This is nearly always advantageous and can save you thousands of pounds in interest payments. Another possibility is an 'offset mortgage' which offsets any savings you have against the mortgage to again reduce the sum you are paying interest on.

If you have the resources to do so, eliminating any consumer debt (particularly as it usually carries much higher interest charges than a mortgage) will reduce your need for income in the future and make for a more comfortable retirement.

If all else fails, you may be able to plan to use the tax-free cash from your existing pensions to mop up any outstanding mortgage and consumer debt.

Managing your lifestyle expectations

In Chapter 8 when we talked about reducing your pension gap from both directions – by increasing your pension as much as you can, but also by reducing your expectations about how much you will need to live on in retirement. On page 74 we introduced the idea of 'trialling', which is basically having a go at living on a lower income and finding out how well you cope.

By using an extended version of trialling in the years before retirement, you can attack your pension gap from both directions. By adjusting your lifestyle now, you make the transition to your retirement income easier to cope with. But also, since you will be living on less, you will have spare cash that you can funnel into pension provision (which will be enhanced by tax relief), or even a retirement contingency fund.

Summary

▎ Think about planning to retire later to take advantage of the pension turbocharger effect.

▎ Now is a good time to make sure you have all the information about the various pensions you have accrued during your career.

▎ Look carefully at the options available to you in your current pension scheme – particularly if you change jobs.

▎ Start thinking about the lifestyle you want in retirement, and start to make adjustments now if you can.

Longer-term planning for retirement (30s and 40s)

If you still have decades to go before your retirement, you are in the fortunate position to take maximum advantage of the power of compound interest to build up a healthy pension. But, as the saying goes, you have to be in it to win it; the most important thing is to make a start, no matter how small. You also need to be aware of the longer-term implications of some of the pension choices you have, particularly when you take a new job.

Even if you are a long way off retirement, it is worth scanning through the previous chapters to get an idea of the things that you will need to face. There is no evidence to suggest that things will improve in future. In fact the continuing decline in birth rates and growth in the retired population suggests that for successive generations the pensions crisis is likely to continue to get worse – there will be fewer working people providing for more pensioners.

As we have already seen in Chapter 3, relying on the State isn't really a viable option – the state pension is simply insufficient for most of us.

So the single most important thing you can do, even at a young age, is to take personal responsibility for your own pensions planning. The rest of this chapter will give you some ideas about how to exercise that responsibility.

'Free' pensions

It's not all bad news though!

When you are close to retirement age it is more difficult to build up a significant pension pot (unless you make huge contributions), because the pot has very little time to attract investment returns.

Conversely, any contributions made into your pension pot while you are young have a long time to grow, and the impact can be enormous. A contribution made one year sooner doesn't look as if it makes much difference now, but by the time you get to retirement it makes quite a difference. That extra contribution adds to the total amount going into your pension, and it also has the greatest effect because it has the longest period to grow. The pensions bought by investment returns are 'free' because they don't come out of your pocket: they are generated by the extra time they have been invested for.

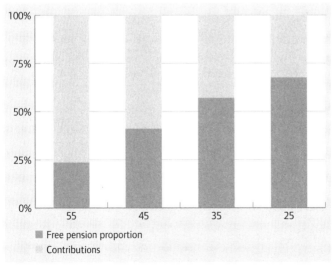

FIGURE 10.1: How investing early generates 'free' pensions
Level yearly contributions from the age shown to age 65. Investment returns 5% per annum.

Figure 10.1 shows the proportion of a pension pot that is effectively 'free' because of the impact of investment returns – assuming a constant level of annual contributions to age 65 and a rate of investment returns of 5% a year.

'Free' pensions for children

Up to £3,600 per year can be saved in a pension tax-free on behalf of children or grandchildren. Putting away the maximum every year from birth to 18 could yield a pension fund of £1.31 million at age 60, for a total net cost to the parent or grandparent of £51,840.

Jobs and pensions

When we consider starting work or changing jobs, we naturally tend to focus on the quality of the job and how much we will get paid.

But as we have seen earlier in this book, company pension schemes play a major potential role in building your own pension pot. So it would be wise to at least consider your new employer's pension provision as one of the factors to be taken into account when accepting a job. During a job interview you obviously need to focus on the job itself, but it's also legitimate to ask questions about pensions because it demonstrates that you are interested in the long term.

Just to give you a guide, here is our rough ranking of the relative attractiveness of different types of company pension schemes:

1. (best) government (or local government or public services) pension scheme;

2. final salary pension scheme funded 100% by the employer;

3 final salary pension scheme with employee contributions;

4 money purchase pension scheme with employer contributions;

5 money purchase pension scheme with employer contributions when the employee also contributes;

6 stakeholder pension scheme with employer contributions;

7 money purchase pension scheme with employee contributions only;

8 stakeholder pension scheme with employee contributions only;

9 (worst) no pension scheme (only possible with less than five employees).

If you are thinking about changing jobs, it's also worthwhile to think about the nature of the pension scheme that you may be leaving behind. All pension schemes benefit from a long and uninterrupted period of membership, because your pension pot is given the maximum scope to grow. Frequent job changes can damage pensions in even the most generous final salary schemes.

Changing jobs

When you change jobs and move from one company pension scheme into another, remember that you have the option to seek a 'transfer value' from your old pension scheme and pay it into your new scheme, or seek enhanced future accrual of pensions rights in your new scheme (or both). You can also explore salary sacrifice, but at a younger age agreeing to an artificially low salary is usually less attractive. These options were all discussed in Chapter 9.

The important point is that you have more room for negotiation at the point you are changing jobs so you should seek to take full advantage of that.

Once you have joined a company pension scheme, you should look at the choices available to you for maximising the growth in your pension pot. If you are offered the chance to make contributions into your pension scheme, you should probably contribute as much as you possibly can. Some schemes offer an 'additional voluntary contribution' (AVC) scheme (see Chapter 5), which is usually worthwhile considering. The sooner you start the better.

More 'free' pensions!

Some employers offer pension schemes where, if you join and contribute, they will make contributions too (often matching your own contributions, for example).

In effect, your employer is offering to give you an extra free pension if you join the scheme. This seems like an offer you simply can't refuse. Sadly, there is evidence that a large proportion of young people don't join these schemes simply because they don't want to make their own contributions. They are building up a massive problem for the future, but simply don't see it now. If you have the chance to join such a scheme, grab it now.

If you find yourself in one of the less attractive pension schemes, or even in a job with no pension at all, you will need to be proactive and set up your own pension. Whatever kind of employment you are in, you can take out your own personal pension and make sure that you get the right level of tax relief on it. Getting expert advice early may cost some money but is likely to be a sound long-term investment.

The 50–50 principle

All this is well and good, but in your early career you are already likely to be under financial pressure, particularly if you have a family and mortgage to support, or student loans to repay. Making pension contributions is probably fairly low on your immediate list of priorities (although if you are reading this book, you must be slightly worried!)

One useful tip is that rather than forcing yourself to make pension contributions now, think about splitting your next pay raise 50–50 between current income and future pension. You don't even need to take out a pension plan at this stage: just put the 50% into some form of savings account (preferably tax-free, like ISAs) where the money will grow. This way, the money will still be available in an emergency but you have started to build a pension pot that you can put into a pension scheme later on.

You can use the same principle when you receive an unexpected windfall – for example an inheritance, an insurance policy maturity or even a lottery win. Treat yourself by all means, but also think about bolstering your pension pot by making an extra contribution.

The point is that starting a pension doesn't have to be a 'big bang' that costs a lot of money; it can be simple and painless. Making an early transition at the start can make the later transition to retirement a lot less painful.

Summary

▌ You can effectively build up 'free' pensions at this stage of your career, whether by investing early or taking advantage of the opportunity to join a pension scheme.

▌ The most important thing is to take an active interest and take the opportunities when they present themselves.

▌ When there is any change in your career, whether a promotion or job change, a few moments thinking about your pension can make a huge difference later on.

part 4

The bottom line

In this section we summarise the key themes for everyone to think about, and make some observations about what is likely to happen with the pensions crisis in future.

Principles for everyone

So far we have explained the nature of the pensions crisis and what individuals at different life stages can do about it. In this chapter we summarise the key themes that are relevant to everyone who is concerned about making provision for their retirement.

Retirement is about your life, not just your pension

As we have said in earlier chapters, expectations of retirement have changed dramatically from the 'pipe and slippers' days to a time of increasing lifestyle choices and the opportunity to fulfil some long-held ambitions. The focus has shifted to retirement as the beginning of a new and exciting phase of life rather than the end of your useful working life. While the primary purpose of this book is to demystify pensions and encourage you to take action, there are several other key factors you will need to consider to manage the transition from work to having a healthy and successful retirement.

▌ Have you thought about what you want to do in retirement?

▌ Do you have a clear detailed vision of what your life will be like?

▌ Do you know how you are going to fund it?

▌ Do you have a plan to transition from work to retirement?

▌ Have you discussed your plans in detail with your husband or wife?

Many people find the transition to being retired to be more difficult than they imagined, especially since it represents such a significant change in the amount of time couples spend together. Yet most people spend more time planning their annual holiday than their retirement!

It is probably best to approach the change as you would any other career decision and think about what it is you get from your job (apart from money) and how you will go about replacing that in retirement. It is a good idea to think about how you will spend your time – paid work, voluntary work, hobbies, travel, etc. and – who you will spend it with. If you are part of a couple, it helps to be clear about how much time you will be spending together, what activities you might do alone, how much travel, etc. so you can both adjust.

The other transition that is sometimes difficult is the loss of status as a result of no longer working; men in particular tend to have a lot of their self-esteem tied to their career, which is another reason to consider how and when you stop work and whether some sort of transition will suit you better than a fixed-point finish date.

There are several organisations which run pre-retirement seminars, which might be a good investment in planning this next phase of your life. (Some of these are listed on our website.) Some employers provide these seminars to employees nearing retirement, so it is worth checking.

The single most important thing you can do is to take responsibility for your own retirement. The reality is that no one else will. The sooner you start making provision yourself, the greater the impact on your pension and ultimate security and comfort in your retirement. Put another way, every moment you delay makes your pension gap larger and more and more difficult to recover from.

Take responsibility

▌ Be willing to take responsibility for your own provision. A rough rule of thumb is you should be contributing half your age as a percentage of salary: so if you are 30 you should be contributing 15% of your salary to your pension.

▌ If your employer has a pension scheme, join it. Do it now.

▌ Don't let the perfect be the enemy of the good. Put away as much as you can as early as you can even if it is less than recommended amounts.

▌ Before you give money away to your family, make sure your own pension is sorted out: otherwise you might be forced to ask for their help later on.

Take advice

Financial matters in retirement are complex and, unless you are very knowledgeable about the financial products available on the market and their tax implications, we recommend that you take professional advice. In Chapter 12 we consider where you can get proper advice, but as an overarching principle this is one of the times you will need advice and even where you have to pay for it: it can make a big difference to your retirement income.

Start as soon as you can

The sooner you begin to invest, the longer the time your money has to grow.

Conversely, delay hurts your pension at all ages, but in different ways. Let's suppose that once you get going, you (together with your employer) manage to put £1,000 net per month into a pension plan.

If you are currently age 55 and have ten years to go before retiring at age 65, delaying for five years might reduce your expected pension from roughly £7,300 a year to £3,400 – a reduction of 54%. You would probably expect this, because you are reducing the number of contributions by half.

But the cost of delay is also large at younger ages. If you are 30, a pension at age 65 of £39,700 for the same contribution of £1,000 net per month would be reduced to £31,000 if you delayed for five years – a fall of 22%. But the amount of pension lost is much greater – £8,700 a year: that's because by delaying, you are losing the contributions that would have the most time to earn the most interest.

Claim your full tax relief

As a basic rate taxpayer you are entitled to 20% tax relief on your contributions to your pension. If you are a higher rate taxpayer you may be entitled to a further 20% relief (see our website for links to the latest rates); this is not deducted at source in a personal pension so you need to make sure you claim it on your tax return. The limits on contributions are now quite high (see Chapter 5), so are unlikely to be a problem for most people.

Some estimates are that 250,000 higher rate taxpayers are missing out on this extra tax relief because they don't claim it.

Expect to retire later

The original pension age of 70 for men was set at a time when, historically, few men survived to this age to claim their pension. So pensions didn't cost that much to provide for. The world has moved on significantly since then, and one of the underlying causes of the current pensions crisis is that we are all living a lot longer. As we have already seen, a man retiring now at age 65 can expect to live another 17 years on average. Naturally, the cost of providing pensions at age 65 (or age 60 for women) in the modern world is much higher.

You can choose to deny reality and insist on retiring at the age you originally had in your mind, but as we have already seen, this is likely to cause financial problems. Alternatively, you can choose to accept the fact that you are likely to have a much longer life and take responsibility for making sure that, as far as possible, you do so in financial comfort.

Turning from the philosophical to the practical, we see that the hard numbers back this up. We have just seen the cost of delay in making pension provision, which obviously means that you can improve your situation by starting as soon as you can. When you combine this with the power of the pension turbocharger, you can make a real difference to your pension gap by planning to retire later. A man aged 30 today can *double* his expected pension for the same contribution level by starting to contribute now (rather than in five years' time) and planning to retire at age 70 (rather than age 65) – from a pension of roughly £15,000 to a pension of £30,000 per year, based on a monthly contribution of £500. (Once again, this doesn't allow for any extra income from employment that may be earned between ages 65 and 70.)

This doesn't just work for the relatively young. A man aged 50 who acts now (rather than in five years' time) and retires five years late at age 70 can actually *triple* his expected pension.

We are not suggesting that you are doomed to the inevitability of continuing in a job that you don't like solely for the purpose of boosting your pension when you retire. The trick is to think about and start planning for this issue early. By doing that, you have a far better chance of navigating into a job that allows you to defer your pension, continue to receive income, and provide job satisfaction all at the same time. Thinking about this in advance will generate many more positive choices than being backed into something unpleasant in response to a short-term financial crisis.

Key points for women

A couple of extra specific points for women:

▌ *Try to avoid disruption to your pension contributions – budget for them as part of starting a family.*

▌ *If you are getting divorced, make sure your husband's pension is considered as part of the assets, particularly if you do not have a lawyer to advise you. As we have mentioned before, it could easily be the biggest asset, more valuable than the family home.*

Debt reduction: the best return in town

These days many people carry a reasonable level of debt in terms of personal loans, car financing and credit card balances. There is often debate about whether it is best to clear the debt or to keep savings intact for a rainy day. Everyone should have an emergency fund to tide them over any short-term fluctuations in finances. (Most advice suggests three to six months' worth of living expenses.) However, from the point of view of overall return, consider this. Most personal debt (credit cards, etc.) carry double digit interest payments; it is not unusual for credit cards to have an APR of 19% or store cards to have APRs of over 20%. Remember you will be financing this debt out of income that you have already paid tax on.

By comparison, you would be doing well in the current climate to get 4% return on savings (whether inside or outside a pension plan). So if you have £1,000 of debt and £1,000 of savings at the same time, you are running at a loss of about 16% a year – £160. You can easily eliminate this loss by switching some of your existing savings to pay off the expensive debt.

Put another way, your return on savings effectively leaps from about 4% to an incredible tax-free return of about 20% a year! That's why reducing your outstanding debts as much as you can without compromising your income position is one of the best things you can do.

Recent research by Age Concern suggests that retirees on average carry £10,000 in debt. If this is you, you stand to gain overall by clearing it down.

Diversification

While a pension is very effective and is the most tax-efficient source of funding your retirement, it is important to take a holistic view of all your assets. The old advice about not keeping all your eggs in one basket is still relevant. You need to consider your other assets and when you may need to access those assets in your retirement.

One major decision is what happens with the family home. For some, it is important to retain the family home for adult children to visit and indeed inherit at some point. For others it is an opportunity to downsize and enjoy both the additional income and the freedom that a smaller place offers. The timing of this decision is also crucial: is it something you want to do in early retirement or is it something you want to leave until later? There are advantages and downsides to both, so it is worth thinking about what you want to achieve.

Children and grandchildren

If you are fortunate enough to solve your own pensions crisis, you might like to think about helping others. Because everyone is entitled to hold a stakeholder pension and get the basic 20% tax relief, you may want to consider helping the next generations avoid a pensions crisis by setting up a pension for them now. Each year you make the maximum stakeholder contribution of £2,880, their pension fund contribution is increased to £3,600 because of the tax relief.

Here is where the power of compounding can really come into its own. If you invested the full stakeholder amount for your child or grandchild at birth to age 18 (£2,880 net a year or £51,840 in total) and then didn't invest anything else but left the fund to accumulate until their retirement at age 65, the fund could be worth close to £300,000 – because of the powerful combination of tax relief and investment returns.

Inheritance planning

Another major decision you might have to make has to do with inheritance taxes. This used to be the preserve of the rich, but, with the rise in house prices over the last two decades, more and more families fall into the inheritance tax bracket and at 40% the tax can make a very substantial dent in your plans for your family. Recent changes in the legislation mean a couple can leave up to £650,000 tax-free (for 2009/2010) but anything above that is taxed at 40%.

The good news is that the experts describe inheritance tax as being largely voluntary: in other words, there are actions you can legitimately take to pass on more of your hard-earned money to your successors rather than to the Treasury. This is a very specialised area, and one where the rules and products available change regularly so if this applies to you, you need to take proper independent advice on your options. Since some of these actions require you to live for a certain number of years to take full legal effect, then the 'sooner rather than later' principle applies.

Unexpected events

As someone once said, life is what happens while you are planning something else. Sometimes life doesn't go to plan and something happens to stop us in our tracks. Here, we deal with some of the more common events and outline briefly the issues that you need to consider.

Job loss

Losing your job can be devastating to your confidence as well as to your finances. What actions can you take?

▍ Try negotiating the terms of your departure with your employer: some employers are prepared to be generous with pension provisions, especially since it is not such an obvious cost to the bottom line. It has been known for employers to grant a generous pension, particularly for those close to retirement – but this is likely to be the exception.

▍ You may want to consider putting some of your redundancy money into your pension fund either in your company scheme or your own personal pension arrangements, particularly if you would be paying tax on it otherwise.

▐ Get yourself on the job market as soon as you can to minimise the gap in your pension contributions.

▐ Think carefully about transferring your previous pension arrangements to a new employer. This is particularly important if you have a final salary scheme. Do not make hasty decisions.

Divorce

With one in three marriages in the UK ending in divorce, it is important to be aware of the implications for your pension. Since 1999, wives and husbands are entitled to an explicit share of the pension assets, so you need to think about what will give you the best outcome. If you are the one with the pension (especially a final salary one), you may want to keep it intact and trade some other assets for it in the short term. This will be especially relevant if your future earnings capacity is high and therefore the value of your pension income when you retire is likely to increase significantly.

If you are the spouse with none or very little pension provision, you need to make sure the pension is taken into account in the settlement and that its value is fairly represented. Despite the change in legislation, less than 12,000 of the 138,000 divorces in 2007 had a 'pension sharing' order (although there will also be many cases where one spouse retains all of the pension and this is balanced by payment of other assets to the other). If you are being advised by a lawyer, he or she should bring this into account – although the valuation of pension assets in these circumstances is notoriously complex.

Death

The critical thing to do when making financial provision in the event of your (or your spouse's) death is to make a will. This is a fairly easy thing to do either through a local solicitor, or by buying a standard form from your stationers or a website. That will ease the practicalities of your death for your family: absence of a will (called 'intestacy') can make dealing with your finances after your death protracted and difficult.

Many pension schemes provide a reduced pension (usually half) for a surviving partner. There is an option to provide this benefit on annuities but the take-up is relatively low. If your spouse would suffer financial hardship without your income, it is best to think about making sure you have adequate cover.

Most company pension schemes also provide some form of life assurance while you are still employed (but not afterwards): you need to check your scheme details to understand what cover you have.

Summary

▌ A recurring theme of this book has been the importance of taking responsibility for your future pension. By being proactive, all the little opportunities to make a difference can be turned to your favour rather than being allowed to dribble away.

▌ Once you have decided to take control, you can apply pension-thinking to all of the different life events that occur.

▌ At all life stages, using the power of the pension turbocharger to retire later is one of the most effective things you can do. Given that increased life expectancy is one of the root causes of the pensions crisis, it is also one of the most logical when taking a 'whole life' view.

Getting advice

12

When we were researching this book, we were surprised by the sheer quantity of information that is publicly available about pensions. In fact, there is so much that it is difficult for an interested person to wade through it all and pick out the bits that are of most relevance.

We hope that this book has gone some way towards highlighting the most relevant and important issues. However, everyone is so unique that we cannot hope to provide information that is tailor-made for your own specific situation. That's why on many occasions we have said that you would be wise to seek out advice.

Although we cannot give you the advice ourselves, we can give you a bit more information about how to go about finding an adviser. In broad terms, there are three main categories of advice, and we will consider each in turn:

1. Advice you don't have to pay for;
2. 'Tied' advice;
3. Independent advice.

Free advice

There is a lot of free information available, and we have listed links to the main sources on the companion website,

www.thepensionscrisis.com. The Financial Services Authority is the main government-sponsored provider of financial information for the consumer, and one of its main tasks is to promote financial education.

While information gives you lots more facts and figures, it does not necessarily tell you what to do if your personal situation is at all complicated (and sadly, for most of us, it is). This requires advice, and you can't really get good advice without the help of an experienced and professional expert.

Advice is much more expensive than information, which is why it is far more difficult to find free advice than free information. The government launched a 'generic advice' initiative in 2007 (also known as the Thoresen report) and this will eventually lead to the introduction of a new 'money guidance' service under the guidance of the FSA and in collaboration with other bodies like the Citizens' Advice Bureau and The Pensions Advisory Service.

Money guidance

The government accepted the Thoresen report's recommendation on money guidance in 2008 and, in partnership with the FSA, is taking forward a pathfinder programme for such a service.

It will cover areas like:

▌ helping people budget their weekly or monthly spending;

▌ saving and borrowing, and insuring and protecting people and their families;

▌ retirement planning;

▌ understanding tax and welfare benefits; and

▌ jargon-busting – demystifying the technical language used in the financial services industry.

The Pathfinder pilot has been launched in the North West and North East of England and will run for 12 months. The national roll-out is expected to start in 2010.

To find out the current status of the money guidance initiative, please check our website. You could also try talking to your local Citizens' Advice Bureau.

'Tied' advice

'Tied' advice can look free because the adviser is being paid by one of the product companies, typically an insurance or investment company. But there is no such thing as a free lunch – you are likely to end up paying for the advice indirectly through the margins and commissions in the products that you buy.

That doesn't necessarily mean that the advice will be bad; you just need to be aware that the adviser is working mainly for the company he or she is 'tied' to, rather than you. And even if the advice looks free, you will probably end up paying for it in some shape or form.

We're not saying you shouldn't use a tied adviser, but you need to do it with your eyes open. You should check that they are properly qualified to give the advice they are giving, and you should make sure you know how much they will earn from each of the products they suggest. (FSA rules require that they disclose this information in a 'keyfacts about the cost of our services' document, but it's up to you to look out for it and check that you are happy.)

Independent advice

The word 'independent' can mean many different things, but for this purpose we use it to mean that the adviser is not tied to any product provider (or group of providers). Independent Financial Advisers (IFAs) have no contractual ties to the product providers (such as life insurance companies) whose products they advise on. They work directly for you.

IFAs are the only advisers who must (under the regulator's rules) provide you with the option to pay for your advice entirely by fee, rather than taking any commission that the product provider will pay. As such, they give you more flexibility when it comes to deciding how you want to pay for the advice you receive.

This has a couple of huge advantages. First, if you agree to pay fees rather than commission they can provide financial advice without feeling the need to sell you a product to generate income for themselves. And second, if they do recommend a product, they can choose the product that best suits your circumstances from the whole market. Their independence enables them to research products from across the whole market.

Information and advice

There is a huge amount of information available about retirement and pensions, whether in newspapers, books (including this one), advertisements and the internet. This information can be helpful in broadening your knowledge, but equally it can be intimidating (because there is so much of it), impenetrable (because of all the jargon) and confusing (because it isn't clear how it affects you personally).

Anyone can give you information.

Advice is different from information. Advice is about understanding your personal circumstances and providing guidance on the decisions and actions that will help you the most. Advice usually includes useful information too (but information cannot include advice). All financial advisers must be authorised by the Financial

Services Authority (FSA). If you are dealing with an adviser who is unauthorised, they are breaking the law and you will not benefit from the protection that authorisation gives consumers. In order to check to see whether or not an adviser is regulated, visit the FSA's central register at: **www.fsa.gov.uk/register**.

By definition, anything that comes from a 'passive' source (like a publication) – even if it sounds like advice – can only ever be information because it has not been tailored to you. There are many firms and organisations who are able to give you information, but they are not regulated by the FSA and they are not giving advice.

If you feel that you need help in making financial decisions around planning for retirement you probably need advice, not just information.

How do I choose an adviser?

First, you need to decide whether you are happy to receive advice from someone who can only recommend the products of a single company (or small group of companies). If that is the case, you can contact the company directly and they will arrange for an adviser to get in touch with you.

If you want to receive advice from someone who works for you rather than a product company and can provide you with advice about the products from any company in the market, you will need to find an IFA (independent financial adviser). Several organisations who promote financial advice can help you find an adviser in your area, and up-to-date links are provided at **www.thepensionscrisis.com**.

Firms must also give you certain information about themselves, their services and their costs. This information will help you shop around.

Most advisers will say that, irrespective of how they get paid, they are acting on your behalf when giving advice. But whichever adviser you choose, it would be wise to be absolutely clear whether they are being paid by you or by the product company. If there is any doubt, ask them directly whether they are an IFA – that is, acting as your agent and providing advice on products from the whole of the market.

Paying for advice

A financial adviser's service is not free. All advisers, whether IFAs or those tied to banks or building societies, charge for their services. Whatever form these costs and charges take, they must be made clear to you at the start.

If the adviser is tied to one particular company, that company will pay the adviser itself (whether in salary, bonuses or some form of commission). You will still be funding this cost through the expense charges that the company makes on any pension plans you purchase from the company.

IFAs operate a fee-charging or commission-based service (or a combination). Many operate a retainer system, charging a figure based on the investments they look after for you. If you decide to pay fees, the adviser will charge you for his services in much the same way that an accountant or solicitor would do so (and probably at comparable rates). Commissions aren't paid directly by you – they are paid by the company whose products you eventually purchase on the advice of the IFA. But as in the case with a tied adviser, you will be paying this commission through the expense charges on the product you purchase.

At present, commission payments have advantages in that they escape VAT (whereas VAT has to be added to fees) and because they come out of your pension you get tax relief on them. Also, many people still prefer paying for their advice indirectly through the commission on products they purchase, rather than have an up-front invoice for fees. Some IFAs combine the payment systems by charging fees, but offsetting these with any commissions received from product providers.

What should I expect from an adviser?

First, you have a right to expect that your adviser is appropriately qualified to provide you with expert financial advice on retirement planning. Not all advisers are qualified to the same level and there are a number of different types of qualifications. The most straightforward way to deal with this is to ask your adviser to confirm in writing that he or she is properly qualified.

Firms that give financial advice based on an assessment of your personal circumstances must only recommend products that are suitable for you. Once they have delivered their advice, an adviser must follow this up in writing, setting out the reasons why they are giving you that advice.

When an adviser recommends a specific pension product, they will give you a Key Features Document about it. The Key Features Document gives details of the product and should answer questions about:

- the aim of the product (i.e. that it is a pension plan);
- your commitment;
- how your payments are invested;
- the main risks;
- the tax implications.

The adviser will also tell you about the fees and charges.

Many IFA clients value the fact that their adviser will continue to stay in contact with them and offer ongoing advice. If this is the service you would find useful, make sure you and your IFA agree the basis on which this will work.

Summary

▌ On occasion, particularly when you have major or complicated decisions to make about pensions, it will be best to get some advice.

▌ There are three main types of advice: generic, tied and independent. Make sure you know which one you are getting.

▌ All advice has to be paid for by someone. If you want advice that is completely dedicated to your own needs, you may have to pay for it.

▌ If you pay for advice, you have a right to expect professional standards of behaviour and service.

The pensions crisis and the future

Pensions are not a passing fad: they have been around for a long time and are an important part of the structure of our lives. In this final chapter we reflect on the pensions crisis and consider the future for pensions in the UK.

In the current economic climate, all the signs are that the pensions crisis on a national level will continue unabated. Historically low investment returns coupled with the rising average age of the population will continue to put pressure on existing pension schemes. We expect the trend of closing of final salary schemes to new members to continue. It is likely that some schemes will also look to reduce the benefits to existing members. One example is a recent decision by a major retailer to either require contributions or restrict the level of salary increase that counts towards final pension. The most common employer response will be a switch to money purchase schemes or the new personal accounts, both of which result in significantly lower pensions to the individual.

So we can no longer leave our own pensions to fate: we have to take control. But for such a simple issue, there is far too much complexity and this becomes a barrier to people who want to take control. To help us overcome this, there is a vast amount of information available from a huge array of sources.

The paradox is that there is simply far too much helpful information for the average person to be able to absorb it all! We don't see any evidence that this unhelpful situation is likely to change in future.

There are a couple of identifiable changes on the pensions horizon.

The emerging crisis in pensions was recognised by the government, who commissioned the Turner report on pensions. This recommended the introduction of a simple basic pension scheme for everyone called 'personal accounts' (see the textbox on p.180 for details).

The last major government initiative on pension products – stakeholder pensions – suffered from the effects of the law of unintended consequences and there is ample scope for personal accounts to suffer a similar fate.

The introduction of personal accounts in 2012 will mean the first level of compulsory pension provision for employers as well as automatic enrolment of employees (although you will be able to opt out). The levels of savings allowed (up to £3,600 a year is proposed) and the expected minimum employer contribution will mean that the people who stand to benefit most are those in lower-paid jobs.

There are already concerns that there may be unintended consequences if employers who are currently contributing more than the minimum proposed in personal accounts reduce their contributions to the new levels. The danger is that most people will believe that if they have taken out the government-recommended pension product, they have done all they need. Contributing to a personal account might reduce the pension gap but not eliminate it, yet most people will not appreciate this.

The second change is relevant for those who are heavily reliant on the state pension. The government has committed to reintroducing the link between state pensions and average earnings (instead of the retail prices index). The price of this commitment is that the age at which you are entitled to the state pension will increase to 68 by 2046.

Personal accounts – the proposals

Personal accounts are intended to solve the problems of low portability and high charges. They will do this by operating as a large, multi-employer occupational pension scheme and extending the benefits of employer schemes to those currently without access to them.

The large scale of personal accounts means that the set-up costs can be spread over a longer period and recovered from higher funds under management, thus reducing the average charge. This large scale will allow personal accounts to achieve economies of scale similar to those of large occupational schemes. However, unlike many employer schemes, individuals will be able to keep their account as they change jobs and continue to make contributions.

The Government estimates that personal accounts could have between 6 and 10 million members with private pension saving of around £8 billion a year, of which approximately 60% will be new saving:

- *individuals will be automatically enrolled if they earn above £5,000;*
- *employees will pay contributions of around 4% on their earnings between approximately £5,000 and £33,500 a year;*
- *the employee contribution will be matched by 3% from the employer together with around 1% in the form of normal tax relief from the State;*
- *the band of earnings on which contributions will be paid will be uprated in line with earnings to ensure the scheme is sustainable;*
- *employees aged over 22 and below state pension age will be eligible for automatic enrolment; and*
- *employees outside these age bands will be able to opt in to the scheme, with access to an employer contribution if they fall within the earnings bands.*

There are some indications that things are getting better for women's pensions.

▌ The falling birth rate and tendency to have children later in life mean women are in the workforce longer and are more established in their careers before having a career break.

▌ Younger women are doing better in education than men and this is likely to lead to higher earnings capacity. Indeed women are expected to account for over 50% of millionaires by 2025.

▌ Women tend to be more concentrated in the public sector. For example, they now account for over half of all GPs in the NHS. The impact of the generous final salary schemes will start to flow through in future cohorts of female retirees.

▌ Legislative changes should improve the pension position of women. The Pensions Act 2007 significantly increases state pensions for many women, by reducing the qualifying period from 39 to 30 years and allowing credit for caring responsibilities. However, it is still expected to be 2025 before we reach equality of provision for men and women.

▌ There is evidence that younger women are taking more responsibility for their retirement than older women.

On the other hand, there are some major issues that show no sign of being resolved in the immediate future.

Public sector pensions

The cost of final salary public sector pension schemes has been increasing substantially in recent years: the cost is currently estimated at close to £1 trillion. While it would be hugely unpopular with public sector employees and trade unions, the government could make substantial savings by altering the funding of these schemes either to less favourable versions of a final salary scheme (using average salary over your working life, for example) or indeed to a money purchase arrangement. There has been press speculation that the government have taken legal advice in this area, so it may be on their agenda.

The Taxpayers' Alliance has obtained figures showing that 17,150 public sector workers have already retired with pension pots worth more than £1 million. The traditional justification was that salaries were lower in the public sector and the pension benefit was therefore justified. However, according to the Office for National Statistics, the average public sector worker earned £25,896 a year in 2007, compared to £22,828 in the private sector. Only the top 20% of private sector workers are paid more than public sector peers.

The case for some form of change, not least to maintain some sort of parity with the private sector, is compelling.

Complexity and confusion

As we have said earlier, pensions are simple. But invariably when you ask a simple question about pensions, you get an incredibly complicated answer – just look at the definition of whether you are entitled to receive the basic state pension.

The Pension Credit calculator on the DWP website is described as 'easy to use and it should take no more than a few minutes to give you an estimate'. This is followed by ten separate screens, on each of which detailed data has to be entered. After all that, it says that 'The calculator will not cover everybody's circumstances'.

Why is this? One of the most obvious underlying causes must be that while pensions are fundamentally long-term, governments change on a much shorter time cycle and almost every new government has felt the need to tinker with the pensions system. Every time the pensions system is changed, people have to cope with an extra layer of complexity by dealing with both the old and the new – and also with the inevitable complex transitional arrangements. Even worse than this, the cabinet responsibility for pensions seems to be fairly junior and rotated at least once every two years – hardly enough time to start to understand the system, let alone make sensible decisions.

So why is this a problem? The pensions system is supposed to be about encouraging people to provide for their pensions. But at a time when much of the population is faced with a pensions crisis and needs to take control to resolve it for themselves and their families, the pensions system has become so complex and intimidating that it has become a major barrier that actually prevents people from taking action.

Entitlement to basic state pension

The basic state pension (BSP) is a flat-rate pension paid to anyone who has paid enough National Insurance contributions or has enough credits when they reach their state pension age (SPA).

Currently, the full rate of BSP is payable if you have qualifying years of about 90% of the years in your working life. This is currently 39 years for a woman and 44 years for a man. Your working life begins at 16 and ends when you reach your SPA. The minimum BSP is payable if you normally have 10 or 11 qualifying years. This is normally 25% of the full rate. The more years you work or have credited then the more BSP you earn.

Women reaching SPA on or after 6 April 2010 will only require 30 qualifying years to claim the full BSP.

A spouse and civil partner who has not paid sufficient contributions to qualify for a BSP in their own right will receive pensions based on their spouse's or partner's contributions when they both have reached SPA. For example, if a woman reaches 60 but her husband is only 62, she will have to wait until he is 65 before she can claim the pension based on his record.

▶

The SPA for men and women is currently 65 and 60, respectively.

Between 2010 and 2020, the SPA for women will increase to 65 to ensure equality. Women born on or between 6 April 1950 and 5 April 1955 are affected by this change.

Between 2024 and 2026, 2034 and 2036 and 2044 and 2046, the SPA for both men and women will rise to 66, 67 and 68, respectively. Those born after 5 April 1959 are affected by these changes.

Our SPA calculator will tell you when you'll be able to draw your state pension.

Left hand and right hand

The enormous complexity of the pensions system and its interrelationship with the benefit, taxation and regulatory systems has created some deep-rooted illogicality.

We already described in Chapter 5 how stakeholder pensions were introduced as a means of encouraging the less well-off to take out their own pensions. However, the margins permitted in these products were so small that pension companies could not afford to promote them to the desired target market. As a result, stakeholder pensions have largely been bought by the better off (and recent pensions simplification has raised the contribution limit from £3,600 to 100% of salary so this trend is likely to accelerate).

The situation is now being compounded, but even more so, with the introduction of personal accounts – again with the intention of encouraging the less well-off to save for a pension. The limit on a personal account contribution is currently set at £3,600 per year, and an average contribution of £1,900 is expected. As we pointed out in Chapter 5, loss of Pension Credit is worth roughly £39,000 to a 65-year-old male. The average person investing £1,900 a year in a personal account would have to contribute for 20 years to get a pension pot of £39,000 (assuming a 5% annual return) and wipe out the prospective loss of Pension Credit – in other words, a return of zero for an outlay of 20 years' contributions. Ironically, this penalty only applies to the people that personal accounts were designed to help – the less well-off.

Summary – and overall conclusions

We hope this book has given you food for thought no matter where you are in the retirement life cycle, and that you now have plenty of ideas about how you can improve your own situation.

Here are some key thoughts that we would like to leave you with:

▍ There is a significant pensions crisis in the UK, caused primarily by increased life expectancy and reduced interest rates and investment returns.

▍ Unless you are fortunate enough to have enjoyed membership of good final salary schemes, it probably affects you. This means that you have a gap between the amount you need in retirement, and the pension you are likely to get.

▍ Remember that this isn't just about money; it's about a major chunk of your future life and how you would like to live it.

▍ There are three main ways to reduce your pension gap (see Figure 6.1 in Chapter 6):

1 Take responsibility for your existing pension arrangements so that you can maximise their impact. Taking the right decisions can reduce your pensions gap significantly without costing you any extra money.

2 Think actively about how much pension you will need in retirement. Don't make sloppy assumptions – take control.

3 Put as much as you can into a pension plan as soon as you can, as long as you will not be caught by the means-test trap (see the previous section). It's almost always the case that the sooner you start the better off you will be.

▍Pensions are simple, but they have been made devastatingly complex by our legislators. We have kept the information in this book as simple as possible to make the key points understandable. Our companion website has links to a huge amount of detailed information should you to want to discover more.

▍Because the rules around pensions have been made so complex, they are easy to trip up on. For any significant decisions in this area, we recommend that you seek out professional advice.

▍The unnecessary mess surrounding pensions doesn't look as if it will be resolved any time soon, partly because it isn't high up enough on the agenda of our elected representatives. When you exercise your democratic right to vote in an election, you might wish to consider raising pensions higher up your list of important issues for the future.

A pensions glossary

Accrual rate The rate at which benefits build up for each year of 'pensionable service' in your final salary scheme: this is often 1/60th or 1/80th.

Actuary A statistician employed by insurance companies who calculates future risks using statistical data from the past.

Actuarial reduction A reduction factor applied if you take a pension earlier than your normal retirement age to reflect the fact that your pension will need to pay out for longer, and with fewer contributions paid in.

Annuity An annuity is an income for life provided by an insurance company in exchange for a pension fund or any lump sum.

AVC Additional voluntary contribution. Some final salary schemes allow you to make voluntary extra contributions to improve your pension fund.

Compounding Compounding is the effect of the interest earned on your savings or investments, which gets magnified because you also get more interest on the interest that has already been added.

Defined benefit (DB) A defined benefit scheme is a pension where the benefits payable to the members are determined by the scheme rules. Final salary schemes are the most common type of DB scheme.

Defined contribution (DC) A defined contribution scheme is a pension where the contributions from employer and employee are invested, and the pension you receive depends on the amount of contributions made and the investment performance over time. It is also called a money purchase pension.

Drawdown Drawdown is where you decide to manage your assets for a period of time with the intention of buying an annuity later on when your circumstances have settled.

DWP Department of Work and Pensions. The government department responsible for pensions.

Endowment A form of insurance policy normally associated with the purchase of a house which pays out the insured amount on the death of the policyholder, or at a fixed date in the future.

Equity release A product which allows you to access some of the equity from your home without having to sell it and move.

Final salary A pension scheme where your pension is a proportion of your final salary – usually 1/60th or 1/80th of your final salary (as defined in your pension scheme rules) per year of service.

Flexible annuity An annuity that allows you to choose the amount of income you take from it (within limits), and decide how it is invested.

FSAVC Free standing additional voluntary contribution. This is similar to an AVC but it is arranged directly by you with an insurance company and is entirely separate from any employer pension scheme.

Group personal pension A personal pension that is a collection of individual policies, but sponsored by an employer who deals with all the administration. You benefit from lower costs and you can take the pension with you if you change jobs.

Immediate vesting Using a lump sum to purchase a pension under which you immediately retire (or 'vest') to take full advantage of tax relief on pension contributions and the ability to take 25% of the pension tax-free.

Impaired life annuity An impaired life annuity offers higher annuity income to those suffering from severe medical conditions likely to reduce their life expectancy.

Investment bond A type of managed investment which provides investors with access to a range of underlying funds.

ISA Individual savings account. An account where your savings or investments accumulates tax-free. Each individual is entitled to contribute to an ISA every tax year, subject to limits.

Lifestyling Lowering the risk profile of your pension investments as you get closer to retirement to lock in gains and minimise exposure to the stock market.

Money purchase A type of pension where your contributions accumulate in a fund which is yours to purchase a pension with when you retire.

Open market option The ability to shop around among insurance companies to get the best pension rates and to buy your annuity from the provider who offers the best price for your pension fund.

Pension annuity An annuity bought by a pension fund as opposed to your own cash.

Pension commencement lump sum (tax-free cash) The proportion of your pension pot you are allowed to take as a tax-free lump sum when you retire – currently 25%.

Pensions crisis The fact that although expectations about our needs in retirement have not diminished, the amount of pension income we are likely to receive has declined, often substantially, as a consequence of people living longer and investment returns being lower.

Pension gap The gap between the pension you think you need to retire on, and the amount of pension you are actually likely to receive.

Pension pot The total amount of money from different sources you will have available to fund your retirement.

Pension price The conversion rate to convert your pension fund into an annuity which provides income for the rest of your life.

Pension sharing When a pension is shared between the spouses as part of a divorce settlement.

Pension sharing order Legal document used to implement the sharing of pensions between spouses in a divorce.

Pension turbocharger The combined impact of a set of factors affecting your choice of retirement age that make the increase (or decrease) in pension much greater than you might expect.

Personal accounts New pension account being introduced by the government in 2012.

Personal pension A personal pension is a policy you personally take out with an insurance company where you are entitled to all the benefits of the policy. It is entirely independent of any employer.

Phased retirement An alternative to buying an annuity, available on some pension products, that enables you to vary the income you take from your pension after retirement.

Purchased life annuity An annuity bought with your own cash. A portion of the annuity income is regarded as a return of your original capital and is therefore not taxed. The remaining income is taxed as normal.

Salary sacrifice A scheme where you agree to take a lower salary in return for a higher contribution to your pension funded by the reduction in both your employer and your own National Insurance contributions.

SERPS State earnings related pension scheme. A scheme that provided an extra state pension on top of the basic state pension. Later renamed the State Second Pension.

SIPPs Self invested personal pensions are a variation on normal personal pensions which allow you to control which investments are purchased by your pension.

Stakeholder pension A low-cost form of personal pension introduced by the government to encourage lower earners to save for retirement.

State pension The state pension is the pension provided by the government to everyone over state retirement age with the relevant national insurance contributions.

Index

Page numbers in *italic* denote a figure